NINA RAINE

Nina Raine began her career as a trainee director at the Royal Court Theatre. She dramaturged and directed the verbatim play *Unprotected* at Liverpool Everyman, winning TMA Best Director Award and Amnesty International Freedom of Expression Award for an Outstanding Production on a Human Rights Theme.

Plays include *Rabbit*, which she also directed, at the Old Red Lion in 2006, transferring to the Trafalgar Studios and as part of Brits Off-Broadway in New York (Charles Wintour Evening Standard Award and Critics' Circle Award for Most Promising Playwright); *Tiger Country* at Hampstead Theatre; *Tribes* at the Royal Court (also in New York, winning an Offie for Best New Play, Drama Desk Award for Outstanding New Play, New York Drama Critics' Circle Award and Off-Broadway Alliance Award; and has been staged worldwide); *Consent* at the National Theatre, in the West End, and broadcast on NT at Home; and *Stories* (also directed) at the National Theatre.

Other directing includes *Shades* at the Royal Court (Critics' Circle and Evening Standard Awards for Most Promising Newcomer); *Longing* by William Boyd at Hampstead; and April De Angelis's *Jumpy* at the Royal Court and in the West End.

Film includes an adaptation of her play *Tribes*.

Nina Raine

BACH & SONS

NICK HERN BOOKS

London

www.nickhernbooks.co.uk

A Nick Hern Book

Bach & Sons first published in Great Britain in 2021 as a paperback original by Nick Hern Books Limited, The Glasshouse, 49a Goldhawk Road, London W12 8QP

Bach & Sons copyright © 2021 Nina Raine

Nina Raine has asserted her moral right to be identified as the author of this work

Cover image by Muse Creative Communications

Designed and typeset by Nick Hern Books, London
Printed in the UK by Mimeo Ltd, Huntingdon, Cambridgeshire PE29 6XX

A CIP catalogue record for this book is available from the British Library

ISBN 978 1 83904 013 9

Bach & Sons was first performed at the Bridge Theatre,
London, on 29 June 2021 (previews from 23 June). The cast
was as follows:

JOHANN SEBASTIAN BACH	Simon Russell Beale
MARIA BARBARA BACH	Pandora Colin
ANNA MAGDALENA WILCKE	Racheal Ofori
CARL PHILIPP EMANUEL BACH	Samuel Blenkin
WILHELM FRIEDEMANN BACH	Douggie McMeekin
JOHANN GOTTFRIED BERNHARD BACH	William Barker
	Teddy Button
	Aidan Hennelly
	Harry Weston
KATHARINA	Ruth Lass
FREDERICK THE GREAT	Pravessh Rana

Understudies

JOHANN SEBASTIAN BACH/ FREDERICK THE GREAT	Nick Barclay
CARL PHILIPP EMANUEL BACH / WILHELM FRIEDEMANN BACH	Al Coppola
MARIA BARBARA BACH / ANNA MAGDALENA WILCKE / KATHARINA	Zara Tomkinson

Director	Nicholas Hytner
Set Designer	Vicki Mortimer
Costume Designer	Khadija Raza
Music Supervised by	George Fenton
Lighting Designer	Jon Clark
Sound Designer	Gareth Fry
Associate Director/ Movement Director	James Cousins

Costume Supervisor	Eleanor Dolan
Props Supervisor	Lily Mollgaard
Wigs, Hair & Make-Up	
* Design Supervisor*	Suzanne Scotcher
Casting Director	Robert Sterne
Production Manager	Kate West

Thanks

Many thanks to Melissa Adeleide, Isabella De Sabata, Donato Esposito, Mark Padmore, Ann Pasternak Slater, Robert Quinney, Craig Raine, Isaac Raine, Moses Raine, and Jack Wakefield.

And to Nick Hytner, who first brought the play into being – in every sense.

I am also grateful to John Eliot Gardiner for letting me watch his rehearsals. His book *Music in the Castle of Heaven*, James Gaines's *Evening in the Palace of Reason*, Peter Williams's *J. S. Bach: A Life in Music*, Nicholas Kenyon's *The Faber Pocket Guide to Bach* and Nancy Mitford's *Frederick the Great* were essential, inspiring reading. I am gratefully indebted to their scholarship.

Stephen Roe's expertise was inexhaustible, meticulous, patient – and above all, humane and humorous.

Igor Toronyi Lalic brought Bach to life for me in vivid contemporary colour during our excitable conversations at concerts and in his kitchen.

Thanks to Angela Hewitt for her musical wisdom, and for playing the entire Goldberg Variations for me in her apartment.

Thanks to Murray Perahia also for playing in his house for me, breaking off occasionally to speak, and to his son Raf for telling me about listening to his father practise through the night – which gave me my first scene.

Lastly. People are quick to patronise Wikipedia, but it was a great and swift additional resource to all the Bach experts I consulted first hand.

Characters

JOHANN SEBASTIAN BACH, *fifties and upwards*
MARIA BARBARA BACH, *his wife, late thirties to early
    forties*
ANNA MAGDALENA WILCKE, *early twenties*
CARL PHILIPP EMANUEL BACH, *from teens to thirties*
WILHELM FRIEDEMANN BACH, *from teens to thirties*
JOHANN GOTTFRIED BERNHARD BACH, *four to seven*
KATHARINA, *Maria Barbara's sister, fifties*
FREDERICK THE GREAT, *thirties*

A Note on the Play

From my conversations with Stephen Roe, I know that Bach would not have composed at the keyboard, but at a desk. The first scene is artistic licence.

I am aware that 'Frère Jaques' is too late for the Bachs, but it was the canon that worked best for my purposes.

When Bach addresses his choir in Act One, Scene Two, they can be imagined. Or Bach can address the audience.

The same is true of the assembled court in Act Two, Scene Four.

This text went to press before the end of rehearsals and so may differ slightly from the play as performed.

ACT ONE

Scene One

BACH *sits at a harpsichord, in a wig, playing meditatively to himself. It is dark – late at night.*

He takes his wig off, scratches his head.

He reaches out, takes a sip from a glass of brandy on the harpsichord.

Continues to play.

He is playing 'Sheep may safely graze'. He pauses occasionally, refines the melody, rewinds and plays a phrase repeatedly – sticking on an ornamentation until he is satisfied and moves on forward through the tune.

MARIA BARBARA, *about six months pregnant, comes to stand on the threshold, watching* BACH, *as he feels his way through the melody.*

BARBARA. Bastian.

　　BACH *stops without turning to face her –*

　　It's keeping Gottfried awake.

　　He finishes the phrase he was playing.

　　It's when you play the same thing again and again. He says he's waiting for you to finish it. He says Mummy my eyes won't close.

　　BACH *plays the resolving phrase.*

BACH. Same here. I need it for tomorrow.

BARBARA. Why?

BACH. The Duke's ordered it for the Duke's birthday. Not his birthday, the other Duke's. Weissenfels'. To play after the

Duke's hunt. Not our Duke. The first Duke. Weissenfels.
He's obsessed with hunting. Both Dukes.

BARBARA. Who's Weissenfels?

BACH. This other Duke.

BARBARA. The fat one?

BACH. They're all fat. The unmarried one. The one who looks
like a great tight-mouthed baby.

BARBARA. Oh, that one.

BACH. Has three Saxon flunkeys who help him do all the
things he has trouble doing any more. Like fellating himself.
He has much better musicians than we do.

He plays the next phrase.

BARBARA. Nice. Very simple.

Beat.

Too simple?

BACH. It's got to be simple because our oboeist is going to
have to play it on the flute and he's multi-talentless. If I can
just get hold of a couple of recorders I'll give them the top
part.

He continues playing.

They said to let my inspiration run free and that the budget is
strictly fifty thaler.

They kiss you, then they fuck you.

*He begins to play the 'B' section – taking the melody into a
minor key.*

BARBARA. Oh. Why make it minor?

BACH. More interesting.

BARBARA. Does it have to be interesting?

BARBARA *shivers, cranes to look in the room.*

The fire's nearly out.

BACH. Give it a blow.

She walks over, blows on the embers, which glow on her face. They dim. She blows again.

BARBARA. No. It's gone.

BACH. Doesn't matter. I don't need the fire. I'm not cold. Go to bed, give Gottfried a cuddle from me.

Beat.

BARBARA. Love. You upset Katharina today.

BACH *stops playing.*

BACH. It's quite hard to do this and talk.

BARBARA. You're incredibly grumpy with her and she has feelings.

BACH. She doesn't have feelings. She doesn't give a shiny shit.

BARBARA. She does have feelings and she's an enormous help. She's wonderful with the children. Especially Gottfried.

BACH. It's Gottfried who's wonderful. With her. I heard him. He's unbelievably patient for a three-year-old.

BARBARA. Can you stop contradicting me? You're always disagreeing and saying there's a better way to do everything.

BACH. That's not contradicting, that's one-upmanship.

Beat.

How did I hurt her feelings?

BARBARA.... You hurt *my* feelings, because she's my sister. Even if she doesn't realise, I can see you're being horrible to her.

Beat.

Come to bed.

BACH *is still. Pause. In the pause we hear the whisper of the violin's question in the Chaconne (at 2:18 in Hilary Hahn's recording).*

It's been months.

Pause. The whisper of the violin's answer.

I need comfort.

In the silence, the violin's question is repeated.

Then – the same answer.

BACH. You don't need comfort.

BARBARA. I do need comfort, sometimes.

He turns around, looks at her. Takes her in properly.

She puts her hand on her bump.

…What if it happens with this one?

Beat.

BACH. Why would it?

BARBARA. Because of the twins.

I wish we'd buried them closer together.

Pause.

BACH. They're safe with God.

Beat.

BARBARA. Come to bed.

BACH. I will.

BARBARA. Please.

BACH. I will.

BARBARA *moves to the door, to leave. He starts to play the first section again. She turns back.*

BARBARA. Will there be singing? In this piece?

BACH. Yes.

BARBARA.…What voice?

BACH *continues playing the major section.*

BACH. For this?... Soprano.

BARBARA, *unseen by him, looks at him sadly.*

...It's good for hope, trust.

BARBARA. Yes.

She continues to look at him as he plays. A soprano voice joins the melody, soaring: 'Schafe können sicher weiden, wo ein gutter Hirte wacht...' – 'Sheep safely graze, where a good shepherd watches...'

ANNA MAGDALENA, *twenties, appears – singing the soprano aria.* BACH *rises from the harpsichord, conducting her – rapt.*

BARBARA *watches, sadly.*

Scene Two

BACH *is conducting his choir of boy singers. They are singing 'Wachet! Betet! Betet! Wachet!'*

He interrupts them in frustration.

BACH. Flat!! Flat flat flat flat flat!

They stop singing.

I know this sounds obvious but you *are* all meant to start at the same time.

All you have to do is sing the right notes at the right time. From the top, please –

BOYS. *Wachet! Betet! Betet! Wachet!*
Seid bereit
Allezeit...

BACH. OK stop! Stop. We've got a balance problem. Trumpet, stop thinking about your solo because it isn't a solo. Play *in* so they can be heard.

I see people yawning. I'm sorry you didn't get your lie-in.

Tenors, that was atrocious, there's a reason the tenor parts are harder, it's because your voices have broken because you've been doing this *longer*, there's no excuse. Also, would you mind not wearing your *sword*.

One of the tenors reluctantly takes it off.

Bass.

The bass looks at him shyly.

You're too fat to sing.

I know. I'm fat. But I don't have to sing.

Well, nothing you can do about it.

Again. Eye contact and really good listening.

They sing. BACH is happier, keeps beating time, speaks as they continue to sing.

Come on, come on, lift up your skirts… I'm beating two you're singing three… be careful, be careful, you've got to be absolutely bang on the money… quietly now, quietly… like a little stained-glass window…

They sing, he beats time, suddenly –

Stop. Stop, stop.

It's like you're all singing with your mouth full. Willy. You *are* singing with your mouth full. Stop eating sweets.

Clarity of the words, please. You need to sculpt it more.

(*Demonstrates.*) 'Beeetet. Beetet' – otherwise it goes for nothing.

You're sounding like St Bernards, try to be Italian greyhounds, *if* you can…

We're running out of time, the old biddies are banging at the door. From the upbeat, bar sixty-nine please –

They sing it again. It sounds terrific and they take it at a pace. BACH chants with them.

'Watch!' – 'Pray!' – Trumpets!

They finish. BACH *looks at them inscrutably, then –*

Better.

Amen.

Scene Three

CARL *sits waiting for* BACH *to start the music lesson.* BACH *is fussing over a pile of music manuscripts.*

BACH. For God's sake. Who the hell put Gottlieb *Muffat* on top of Telemann?

CARL. Mum asked me to tidy up in here.

BACH *fussily rearranges the manuscripts.*

BACH. You *can't* put Muffat on top of Telemann. Muffat is a mediocrity. Telemann is not. Telemann has to go on *top* of Muffat.

CARL. Who cares?

BACH. *I* care. There has to be order. In all things.

CARL. Right. (*Ironically gestures to a chaotic heap of notes.*) What's *this*?

BACH. My application to the council for funding.

He gathers it up grumpily.

Have you any idea how long I've spent on that? Even if we *get* the money, they will have had their money's worth, in man hours.

BARBARA *comes in with a newborn baby in her arms, looking around for something.*

Muffat –

He demonstrates –

At the *bottom* of the pile. Telemann at the top. Muffat on top
of Telemann – sacrilege.

He picks up some more scraps of paper.

What the hell *is* all this crap? 'One green two yellow three
right four left'? Is it a riddle?

BARBARA. Ah. (*Takes it from him.*) No, it's crap. His crap.
What colour it is, green or yellow. And which sides he's fed.
I wish they'd stop being green, I don't think it's healthy.

BACH. What did you do with my quill?

BARBARA. I can't remember. Have you seen his blanket
anywhere?

BACH *throws it at her and she deftly catches it.*

Thanks.

She looks around the room.

Bit messy in here, isn't it?

BACH. Whose fault is that? People coming in here stealing
quills, putting Muffat on top of Telemann…

BARBARA *goes out again, humming a tune.* BACH *shuffles
some papers.*

Where the hell is Willy?

CARL. I don't know.

BACH. Well, we can't hang around any longer, I've got
auditions at three. So, your composition from last week.

CARL *eagerly readies himself to listen.*

While we do this, let's not waste time, you can restring this –

BACH *hands* CARL *a violin, looks at the sheet music.*

I asked for a fugue, it is a fugue.

I gave you the subject.

He sings it.

Fourteen notes long. Second voice joins with your answer.

He sings it.

Then the problems begin. Technically, it's all correct. You observe all the rules. Third voice enters, then fourth. But, Carl, they've all got to speak equally.

CARL. But –

BACH. You're favouring your second voice.

CARL. I'm not.

WILHELM (*from off*). *Coming! I'm coming!*

Noises from off – WILHELM *comes in, settles himself.*

BACH. Which is a bit of a cheat. Willy, you're late.

(*To* CARL.) No, your other voices are just treading water. Subservient. Much harder to make each voice equal. They should each have their own integrity, validity. Like a trifle, the layers of cream and jelly have to work wherever you choose to cut it.

He demonstrates on the harpsichord, playing the 'subject' he sang before –

Horizontally, each melody following its own path – and –

He plays a chord –

Vertically, the sum of *all* the melodies together at any given moment, meaning –

CARL. But what's wrong with making one voice win, if it sounds more beautiful?

We hear BARBARA, *singing to the baby, off.*

BACH. Then just write a tune and have done with it. – Wilhelm, why are you late?

WILHELM. I was helping Mummy with the baby.

BACH. No, you weren't, she just came in here. Don't fib, please.

He turns to CARL *again.*

The whole point is to combine two complementary or contrasting thoughts *in the same moment.* Two *feelings* in the same moment. Carl? Are you listening?

CARL. Yes.

Of course I am.

BACH. Are you bored? Or worried? Happy? Or sad? Angry? Or miserable? Or all of them at once?

Pause. We hear BARBARA, *still singing to the baby, off.*

CARL. I don't know.

BACH. Exactly. *That's* what you can do with counterpoint.

BARBARA *continues to sing.* BACH *listens. He speaks to himself.*

Hope filled with pain.

Love filled with irritation.

Et cetera.

Pause. BACH *leafs through another manuscript.*

(*To* WILHELM.) Right. Wilhelm. For a start, I don't know why you immediately went into B-flat minor. And then stayed there for ages. B-flat minor is like black paint. Only for the moments of the most profound grief and despair. Christ on the cross. Don't overuse it.

WILHELM. But I felt like it.

BACH. What, suicidal? Break the rules when you know them properly. Also, I've told you a thousand times, mark in your ornamentation.

WILHELM. But Dad, everyone knows how to fill in. You don't have to write down every last twiddle.

BACH. Do you want other people putting their twiddles all over your stuff?

WILHELM. I wouldn't mind.

BACH. Yes, you would.

WILHELM. I wouldn't.

BACH. You would.

WILHELM. I wouldn't.

BACH. Well, you *should*. You have to look *after* your music.

He gestures around them.

Why else do you think I'm working my hairy little tits off… making copies of all this stuff… with all the bloody ornamentation written in? To hand it on, when I die, to *you*, ungrateful bastards, so you can hand it on to your children, so they can hand it on to their children… precious little thanks I get for it…

CARL. But you're *never* going to die.

BACH. I tell you what, in my case, death would be a great career move. They'd say Bach, him, he was interesting, let's look at him again…

He looks at WILHELM's *manuscript again.*

I digress… skip to the end… re-entry of the subject in a different voice as well as modulating back to the tonic.

Well, you've got nothing of the sort. You only get to the tonic in the last gasp.

WILHELM. I was going to earlier, but then I thought, why?

BACH. To give a sense of resolution, to requite the melody. You delay it until it's almost too late.

WILHELM. It felt boring when I tried.

BACH. It's not. A fugue is a dramatic narrative. You would hear the same melody differently because of everything that's happened in between. It has to come home.

WILHELM. But *you* don't, always.

BACH. No. I take liberties. It's a different thing. And I find justification for those liberties. Whereas you…

He looks at it again.

It's completely off the wall. It's so crumbly, you're skating around all over the place – sometimes I'm not even sure what key you're in.

He studies it.

Thing is, Wilhelm, this isn't a fugue at all. I don't know what it is, but it's not a fugue.

Grudgingly –

It's interesting. Worth keeping. I'm going to put it on The Pile.

He does so. CARL *flinches.*

CARL. Dad!

BACH. But –

CARL. Dad, that's not *fair*! He wrote it in five minutes!

WILHELM. Shut *up*.

CARL. I spent *ages* on mine.

BACH. *But*, I think we need to go back to basics. One voice, and the encouragement of echoes.

(*Calls*.) Barbara!

BARBARA (*shouts from off*). *Hang on a minute!*

BACH *huffs impatiently.*

BACH. *Barbara!!*

BARBARA. *I'm coming!! Hang on a minute!*

BACH (*shouting*). *We need you!! Now!!* – Willy's was more interesting, Carl, yours was more correct, but *neither* of you wrote a proper fugue. Each voice must be formed from the same basic material, and yet, as it enters, make its own independent contribution to the musical argument. – *Barbara!!* – Harmoniously. As a family.

CARL. What family is *that*?

BACH. The woman is painfully slow! – And until you manage that, it's not a fugue.

BARBARA *comes in.*

BARBARA. Can you not be so bloody impatient? You're the most impatient man I know.

WILHELM. Except when it comes to making music. Then he's got the patience of an *insect.*

BACH. Let's get on with it.

(*Sings.*) 'Frère Jacques, frère Jacques…'

He motions to WILHELM. WILHELM *starts to sing.*

WILHELM. / Frère Jacques, frère Jacques…

BACH. / 'Dormez-vous, dormez-vous…'

He gestures at CARL, *who obediently starts to sing.*

CARL. // 'Frère Jacques, frère Jacques

BACH. // 'Sonnez les matines, sonnez les matines…'

WILHELM. // 'Dormez-vous, dormez-vous…'

BACH *gestures at* BARBARA, *who sings.*

BARBARA. /// 'Frère Jacques, frère Jacques…'

CARL. /// 'Dormez-vous, dormez-vous…'

BACH. /// 'Din don din, din don din.'

WILHELM. /// 'Sonnez les matines, sonnez les matines…'

They continue to sing without BACH –

BARBARA. // 'Dormez-vous, dormez-vous…'

CARL. // 'Sonnez les matines, sonnez les matines…'

WILHELM. // 'Din don din, din don din…'

Then without WILHELM –

BARBARA. / 'Sonnez les matines, sonnez les matines…'

CARL. / 'Din don din, din don din.'

Then BARBARA *alone –*

BARBARA. 'Din don din. Din don din.'

She looks around at them, smiling with pleasure.

CARL (*flatly*). It was only harmonious because we were all singing the *same* thing. What *you* were singing.

WILHELM. Plus, it was a canon. Not a fugue.

BACH. Back to basics. As I said. You need to know the rules before you break them.

WILHELM. Four lines, five lines, six lines – I can *do* it, I just can't be bothered. It leaves me cold. Why not wiggle on one line?

BACH. Willy, Willy, Willy. You're being a typical adolescent. Every line has another turn, another door, another direction, endless precipices, endless suspensions, it's geometrical, it's beautiful. Why would you want to stay inside one room?

WILHELM. Why would you want that mad ten-line stuff? It just sounds jangly to me.

BACH. Because you're not doing it well enough. – Also, rules *provoke* expression, they challenge your ingenuity. It's like number patterns. No one can *hear* them. No one can hear that there are 1,283 notes in my first prelude and fugue, 1 being A, 2 – B, 8 – H and 3 – C, making B-A-C-H.

CARL. Except it doesn't, it makes A-B-H-C. 'Johann Sebastian Abhc.'

BACH *pooh-poohs this.*

BACH. Don't be a pedant.

WILHELM. Pedant's calling the pot black.

BACH. The point is, if you're the one making it *happen*, you just go – Hm! Nice!

CARL. But, Dad, you're the *only* one going 'Hm. Nice.'

BACH. Doesn't matter.

CARL. It's doodling.

BACH. You can start with a doodle and end with something mighty. You don't have to be *enslaved* by it. It just stops things getting – glib.

BARBARA. I think it *is* glib.

BACH. What?

BARBARA. Oh all those number games. They're so boring and smug. It's superstition, darling, *really*. It's a form of magic. All those fourteens in your work. You could do it all without that. It's like crossing yourself or counting magpies or touching wood.

BACH. Nothing wrong with touching wood! (*Hastily touching the harpsichord.*) We need all the help we can get.

BARBARA. You're *so* superstitious.

BACH. I'm not superstitious. Apparently it works even if you don't believe in it.

BARBARA. If it helps you, fine, all I'm saying is, don't expect anyone else to appreciate it.

BACH. Oh I *never* expect *that*. I don't do it for an audience.

BARBARA. Yes, I know you always say that, but –

BACH. You have to do it for itself. For God.

BARBARA. Well of course it's for God, but it's for you too.

BACH. It's for God.

CARL. Then why do you care so much about how good your *singers* are? God can read music.

BACH. Because I want it to be the best it can. For God.

There is a disbelieving silence.

KATHARINA *comes in.*

KATHARINA. The first singer's here. To rehearse.

Abruptly, BACH *becomes sullen.*

BACH. All right. Thank you.

> KATHARINA *waits*.

I'll come in a minute.

> KATHARINA *waits*.

Go and tell them I'll be with them in a minute. Please.

> KATHARINA *goes*. BARBARA *waits for a second, then* –

BARBARA (*whispering*). Why do you have to be so *short* with her?

BACH (*whispering*). I'm not.

BARBARA. Poor Katharina, she's ill.

BACH. The woman is like sand. Grit.

BARBARA. She's just doing her duty.

> *Their voices quickly rise.*

BACH. It's called sulking.

CARL. Don't shout at Mum.

BACH. I'm not shouting, / I'm whispering!

BARBARA. / Of course she's going to sulk if you're rude to her!

BACH. I wasn't rude to her! I was perfectly polite!

WILHELM. Stop shouting at Mum!

BACH. / *She's* shouting at *me*!!

CARL. / Dad!

BARBARA. / For God's sake, take a leaf out of your Well-Tempered Klavier!

BACH. I won't be told how to behave in my own house!

WILHELM *and* CARL. *Don't shout at Mum!!*

BACH (*booming*). Then don't tell me how to behave in my own house!!

ANNA MAGDALENA *comes in. They all look at her.*

CARL. Din don din.

ANNA. I'm sorry. Shall I come back?

Beat.

BACH. No, we've almost finished.

Beat.

BARBARA. You're here to audition?

ANNA. No, to rehearse.

BARBARA. Oh dear, Bastian, you double-booked yourself. I thought you had auditions at three.

BACH. No. Not double-booked.

ANNA (*an introduction*). I sing at the court.

BARBARA. Yes, I know who you are, I saw you singing. 'Sheep may safely graze'.

ANNA. Oh!

BARBARA. Beautifully.

ANNA. Thank you.

BACH *starts to shuffle papers together.*

BACH. Right. We'd better get on.

ANNA. And you have been blessed.

BARBARA. Blessed?

ANNA. With a new baby.

BARBARA. Well, I don't know about blessed. He cries. Has a lot of wind.

BACH. We're hoping he'll be a trombonist.

WILHELM. What are you going to rehearse?

BACH. A cantata.

BARBARA. For the court?

BACH. No, church. For Palm Sunday. The boy sopranos aren't good enough.

Beat.

CARL. But –

BACH. It's all right. I'll put her in the organ loft. No one will see it's a woman singing.

BARBARA. No, Bastian –

BACH. What I've written needs a good singer. I'm fed up with having to use amateurs.

CARL. Dad –

BACH. It'll be fine.

BARBARA. Darling.

BACH. I'm not discussing it.

Beat.

WILHELM. You sang in the organ loft once, didn't you, Mummy?

BARBARA. Years ago. When I was thinner. It caused an enormous amount of trouble.

Beat.

ANNA. I'll wait outside.

BACH. There's no need.

ANNA. I interrupted a lesson?

WILHELM. Yes. Dad was teaching us counterpoint.

ANNA. Ah. Lovely. Where complementary thoughts can combine.

CARL. Or *contrasting* thoughts.

BARBARA. Yes.

WILHELM. Dad said I should have modulated back to the tonic sooner. I left it unresolved for too long.

Pause.

(*To* BACH.) Do you want us to go now?

Beat.

BACH. / Yes.

BARBARA. / Bastian, is it really a good idea to let – sorry – (*Gestures at* ANNA.)

ANNA. Anna.

BARBARA. Sing in the organ loft. You've only just got *out* of prison.

BACH. No one will ever know.

But the BOYS *explode, delightedly.*

WILHELM. Daddy was in *prison*?!

CARL. So *that's* where you were all last month!

BACH (*sarcastically, to* BARBARA). Well done. (*To* ANNA.) A technicality. A slight disagreement with my previous employer. A nothing. Four weeks. (*To the* BOYS.) And I made good use of the time. Wrote some studies for organ. In fact I got a hell of a lot more done in there, than here.

CARL. Ha! Banging on about the *rules* of counterpoint, you can't even stay out of prison!!

BARBARA. Well, your father has a problem with authority. Always has done.

BACH. Can you stop *discussing* me, please?

WILHELM. What did you *do*?

BACH. It doesn't matter.

CARL. It does, we want to know.

BARBARA. He couldn't keep his mouth shut.

BACH (*addressing* ANNA *again, ignoring his family*). I can only apologise for my family's lack of decorum in the presence of a guest. In explanation. My previous employer – Duke Ernst – did not wish me to leave my job in Weimar. I desired to accept my current post here in Köthen.

BARBARA. So you went ahead and did exactly what you wanted.

BACH. My situation became untenable. If I am treated unfairly, I will complain. Which I did.

BARBARA. Yes. At the same time as accepting the post in Köthen and trying to bugger off without telling anyone.

You know what he was charged with on arrest? 'For Stubbornness.'

The FAMILY *and* ANNA *cannot help laughing at this.*

It's not even the first time he's been in prison.

BACH. For God's sake!!

BARBARA. Admittedly, it was years ago. An altercation with a bassoonist. He stabbed him.

CARL. You did what?!

BACH. It was only a little prod.

BARBARA. With a knife.

BACH. He played very badly.

BARBARA. My sister had to testify for him.

BACH. And has disapproved of me ever since. Right, you can all get *out* now, we need to rehearse.

BARBARA *and the* BOYS *reluctantly gather themselves.*

ANNA. I'm so sorry to have interrupted your lesson.

WILHELM. Don't be.

As they leave –

ANNA. I'm sure it must be a privilege to be taught by such a great man as your father. You are very lucky.

She turns to BACH.

Are they competitive? It must be hard to teach them together.

BACH. No. It's not hard. In music only honesty counts. You have to be honest or there's no improvement. (*Bluntly.*) At the moment, he – (*Re:* WILHELM.) is better than him – (*Re:* CARL.)

There is a hurt pause, then CARL *throws the violin on the floor with a twang, runs out.* WILHELM *turns on his father.*

WILHELM. Don't say that.

It's horrible.

BACH. Why? You should be pleased.

WILHELM. Bastard –

WILHELM *bursts into tears and runs after* CARL.

BACH. My God, what's wrong with the pair of them?

BARBARA *turns on* BACH, *coldly furious.*

BARBARA. Why did you have to say that?

BACH. Say what?

BARBARA. That Wilhelm is better than Carl.

BACH. Because it's true. At the moment.

BARBARA. Why do you have to favour Wilhelm?

BACH. I don't. He's just better.

I have to be honest.

BARBARA. *Why?* Carl tries so desperately to please you.

Beat.

What's wrong with a little white lie, now and again?

Pause. The baby starts to cry, off.

I'll leave you to your rehearsal.

She stares coldly at ANNA *and* BACH.

Or is it an audition?

I forget.

She leaves. Music – Prelude No. 6 in D minor (The Well-Tempered Klavier Book I).

Scene Four

CARL *is sitting up in bed,* BARBARA *is sitting with him. Nearby, a littler boy,* GOTTFRIED, *lies in bed. He is sick. In another part of the stage,* BACH *sits at his desk, silently writing a score. In another part of the stage,* KATHARINA *quietly folds laundry.*

CARL. What do you think is wrong with Gottfried?

BARBARA. He's doing the right thing. Sleeping will make him better again.

CARL. Is he still hot?

BARBARA *feels* GOTTFRIED*'s forehead. Beat.*

BARBARA. He is still hot but that's not a bad thing. It means his body's fighting it.

CARL. How did he catch it?

BARBARA. I don't know. Maybe when we got wet playing with the hens in the rain. Go to sleep.

CARL. I can't.

Pause.

BARBARA. Where's Wilhelm?

CARL. He went for a walk.

BARBARA *tuts.*

BARBARA. Now?? What does he think he's doing? Where?

CARL. He said he wanted fresh air.

BACH *now starts to play on the harpsichord. Prelude in C major. Pause.*

BARBARA. Listen. The prelude touches as many notes as possible to check that they're all in tune.

They listen.

Daddy is going to do one in every single key.

CARL. That makes... twenty-four.

BARBARA. That's right.

Pause.

CARL. He said he was doing it for Wilhelm. To make a book for him.

BARBARA. Yes.

CARL. Why?

BARBARA. Because Wilhelm is the oldest.

Pause.

There is a natural temperament for each key. F-sharp can be G-flat except it isn't, quite. Each key is a little bit different. Like all of you. Wilhelm, and Gottfried...

CARL. And Katharina...

BARBARA. Yes, and Katharina,,,

Beat. Elsewhere, KATHARINA *moves on to a different pile of laundry, sighs.*

CARL. Katharina is...

BARBARA. Katharina is happy... living her life... in a minor key.

She goes back over to GOTTFRIED, *to check on him again.*

CARL. Why is Katharina not married?

BARBARA. I don't know.

Beat.

CARL. What's Dad?

BARBARA. Difficult to say. A mixture. That's why he's so interesting.

Beat.

CARL. Does he love us all the same?

BARBARA. Of course he does. Differently, but equally.

Pause.

Sweetie, are you all right?

CARL. What colour was my hair when I was little?

BARBARA. Red.

Beat.

You were a very fiery, very temperamental little redhead.

And then, it completely disappeared. When you were about five. It went dark. Whereas Wilhelm was always very blond.

Pause.

CARL. Will God look after Gottfried?

Beat.

BARBARA. Yes. Of course he will.

CARL. Is God cruel?

BARBARA. Of course not, darling.

CARL. Is Dad cruel?

BARBARA. Heavens! No.

Beat.

The tougher he is with you, the more it means he loves you.

CARL. God, or Dad?

BARBARA....Both.

CARL. F-sharp is G-flat. Except it isn't.

Beat.

BARBARA. The thing you always have to remember is that Daddy was an orphan. His parents died when he was nine years old. That's why he loves rules so much – because they make him feel safe. And that's why he hates rules, because he grew up without them.

Beat.

It's like the way he's obsessed with people being on time... but he's always late.

CARL. Isn't that just being a hypocrite?

They listen to BACH *playing.*

It sounds so gentle. But he's not.

BARBARA. He is. Inside each note all the other notes exist.

CARL. He's mean to you.

BARBARA. No.

He loves me.

WILHELM *comes in.*

Wilhelm, get into bed right now. Where were you?

WILHELM. I went out for a walk.

BARBARA. I was worried. Don't do that again, please.

She gets up.

I m going to go and make Guttfried a drink. Please, go to sleep now. Both of you.

She goes out. The BOYS *sit on their beds, listening to* BACH *play. Now he has moved on to Prelude No. 8.*

WILHELM. He's going through all the keys.

CARL. Yes.

Beat.

You stole rum again.

WILHELM. No I didn't.

CARL. Don't lie. You stink of it.

Beat.

WILHELM. Not rum. Gin. Brown gin.

CARL. Idiot. There's no such thing as brown gin. It's called brandy.

He walks over to WILHELM'*s bed and punches him on the arm, hard.*

WILHELM. Ow. Don't hit me.

CARL. Don't steal, then.

WILHELM. Why do you care?

> CARL *lies back down on his bed. They listen to the music.*

CARL. Gottfried was talking in his sleep. He said 'Bye bye, Mama. Bye bye, Papa. Bye bye, Gottfried.'

> *Pause.*

WILHELM. It's a new moon tonight.

CARL. Did you see it through glass?

WILHELM. No.

CARL. Did you wish on it for Gottfried to get better?

WILHELM. Yes.

CARL. Good.

> *Pause.*

WILHELM. I'm going to sleep now.

> *They lie there.*

CARL (*sleepily*). I think that keys are literally… keys. They open doors into different rooms.

> BACH *continues to play, but the piece changes – the harpsichord accompaniment to the Double Violin Concerto in D minor, Largo – and the other instruments join.*

Scene Five

The other instruments fade away, leaving only BACH *playing,
sitting at the harpsichord, with* GOTTFRIED *on his knee.*
GOTTFRIED *is silent, sucking his thumb. Nearby,* BARBARA,
CARL *and* WILHELM *decorate the Christmas tree.* BACH *is
still idly playing his Double Violin Concerto on the
harpsichord.*

BACH....And even the sun and moon make music. The music
of the spheres. And the only reason, Gottfried, that we can't
hear it, is because we have been hearing this music from the
moment we are born...

BARBARA *(thoughtfully)*. Is that your slow movement you're
playing?

BACH....A beautiful music between the heavenly planets.

CARL. And fairies really exist.

WILHELM. Oh, I think it's a lovely idea.

BACH. I'm not making this stuff up. Boethius – no, let's start
with Pythagoras.

Meanwhile BARBARA *has finished rooting around in a box
and has started lighting the stubs of candles in their holders
on the tree.*

BARBARA....We need to use up all the old ends from last
year...

BACH. Where's that bloody violin...

BARBARA looks at the tree, critically.

BARBARA. There's a big gap, right there. With no decoration.

*BARBARA roots through the box again, looking at
decorations critically. Meanwhile* BACH *picks up a violin
and demonstrates.*

BACH. Pythagoras: the pitch of a musical note is in inverse
proportion to the length of the string. *(Plucks the string.)*

Here's the note. Halve the length – (*Plucks it again.*) octave.
And two thirds – (*Plucks it again.*) perfect fifth.

WILHELM. And so what?

BACH. Well, these same musical proportions are found in the
distances between the orbits of the planets. (*To*
GOTTFRIED.) So, they're making music too, my love.

CARL. Sounds like waffle to me.

BARBARA (*of the tree*). We need to *put* something there. Carl,
what do you think. You're good at it.

CARL. Another candle.

BACH (*haughtily*). A world as orderly as this cannot have been
created by chance alone. (*To* GOTTFRIED.) And that should
be a great comfort to you when life seems unfair. Like when
you're not allowed two helpings of Katharina's pudding. Or
when Gottlieb Muffat gets all the jobs.

> WILHELM *and* CARL *laugh despite themselves.*
> BARBARA *holds up a half-burnt candle.*

BARBARA. These really are only stubs. (*Surveying the tree.*)
Now, we should sit here in the dark, and wait for them all to
burn down before we light the new ones. (*A bright new
thought.*) We can each choose a stub, and see which burns
down last. And that stub is the winner.

BACH (*to* WILHELM). It'll happen to you too, Wilhelm. Don't
you worry. In time. You'll be told by some mediocrity that
your compositions range too far harmonically to be decent.

BARBARA. I think that one up there will be the last to go.

WILHELM. I'm choosing this one here.

> BARBARA *blows out the other lamps in the room so the
> room is now lit only by the candles on the tree. The* BOYS
> *settle themselves.*

CARL. Where's Katharina?

BARBARA. She's with the baby. She's worried he's coming
down with something. He's absolutely fine. I think he's
teething.

WILHELM. Look, that one's nearly gone out already.

BACH (*to* GOTTFRIED*; starts to play chords*).... You see,
    Gottfried. Music is evidence of God's divine order in this
    world. And music can also illustrate that divine order.

WILHELM. Does that make you a seamstress of the cloak of
    stars, then?

BACH. Bugger off.

    CARL *studies them ironically.*

CARL. Gottfried really is your ideal pupil. Utterly silent, and
    keeps his thumb in his mouth at all times.

BACH (*ignoring this, he starts to play the harpsichord with*
    GOTTFRIED *on his knee*). Don't listen to them, Gottfried.
    Music is a wonderful language. It can tell you a story. You
    can ask a question. (*Plays some notes.*) You can say
    something secret. (*Plays more notes.*) You can tell the story
    of Christ. (*Plays more notes.*) Descending notes for when he
    is cast down.

CARL. Or asleep.

BACH. Ascending notes for when he is risen.

CARL. Or full of pride.

BACH (*plays more notes.*). Dissonance resolved into harmony.

CARL. Dissonance for the heart of the sinner. And rippling
    scales for flights of angels.

BACH (*sharply*). Wait till you can do it before you sneer at it.
    Of course you can be obvious and reductive. Or you can go
    somewhere interesting. (*Keeps playing.*) Down into the flat
    keys for his misfortune, when Judas went to the priests and
    said, What will you give me if I betray him to you? Falling
    diminished seventh for falsity. They paid him thirty pieces of
    silver. And from that moment he began to look for an
    opportunity to betray him. And Jesus said to his disciples,
    The one who has dipped his hand into the bowl with me will
    betray me. Peter said to him, I will never desert you. Jesus
    said to him, Truly I tell you, this very night, before the cock

crows twice, you will deny me three times. E minor – the
key of despair.

CARL. Dad's version of a bedtime story.

WILHELM. Well, you can't get a much more complex
father–son relationship than God and Jesus…

BACH (*ignoring this*). And Judas kissed Jesus. Then they came
and laid hands on Jesus and arrested him. And the high priest
said to him, Tell us if you are the Messiah, the Son of God.
And they cried, Save yourself, if you are the Son of God.

BARBARA (*warningly, in an undertone*). Don't, darling. He's
too little for it.

Beat.

BACH (*plays from dissonance to harmony*). You see, Gottfried?
You hear that dissonance? It wants to be resolved. Luther got
it. Music is there to serve God. Sermons in sound.

CARL. Well, it gets them into church.

BARBARA. Shh, Carl.

CARL. Gets people feeling emotional. It's a great tool. I feel
very emotional in church. But maybe it's just the music. It all
depends what you think music is for.

BACH. It's there to serve religion. To illustrate the Scriptures.

WILHELM. But everything you just played to Gottfried – it
could have just as easily been about dragons. When you play
something, it can mean one thing to me and something
completely different to you.

BACH. That's why we have the words.

CARL. What about when you don't have words?

Why does music have to *mean* anything? Can't it just be
beautiful?

BACH (*gently*). Carl. You're thinking far too literally. A melody
loves to go somewhere far, far away, and not know how it'll
find its way back. And so it can mirror the chaos of life, sin,
guilt, *doubt*. The whole point is, music can do anything. But,

at the end of it all, the meaning of music is always God. Because God is everything.

Beat.

WILHELM. Then why are you writing cello suites for Prince Leopold?

BACH *gets up from the harpsichord restlessly.*

BACH. Because I've got to feed you lot. Anyway, I can praise God in *them* as much as I like, he'd never notice. He doesn't notice anything. Unless it has tits. I've got to go to Karlsbad with him next month.

BARBARA. Karlsbad? Why?

BACH. A spa trip.

BARBARA (*downcast*). Oh. Another one? What a shame. How long?

BACH. Don't know. It depends how much fun he's having. Those suites will knock their socks off.

BARBARA. I think you should write your Passion. It's obviously on your mind.

BACH. Unfortunately Prince Leopold doesn't want a Passion. He wants to have a good time.

CARL. I thought you were writing dances. That's what it sounded like.

BACH. I'm killing two birds with one stone. Or ten. Each cello suite has two minuets, two bourrées, and two gavottes. Ending with a gigue.

BARBARA. You greedy pig!

BACH. The gigue – now that's a great dance. It can do anger, pride, lust, flirtation…

WILHELM. All in praise of God.

BACH. Oh, shut up. I'll reuse it. I'm always turning things back into church stuff. In fact that's the point. The one *is* the other. Water into wine.

CARL. Means you get paid twice for it, too.

WILHELM. But *dances*?

CARL (*curiously*). Let's have a look at them then.

BACH. On top of the harpsichord there.

CARL *goes over to it*.

BARBARA. Your father is obsessed with dancing. Always has been.

CARL. Shame he's so fat.

BACH. Hey. I used to be slim as a knife, waist like a girl. When I walked to see Buxtehude –

The BOYS *groan and interrupt in unison*.

WILHELM *and* CARL. 'When I walked to see Buxtehude in Luuuubeck...'

Then they sing – back and forth.

CARL. 'I wore out two pairs of boots' –

WILHELM *and* CARL (*a chorus*). 'When I walked to Lübeck.'

WILHELM. 'I was chubby, lost two stones' –

WILHELM *and* CARL. 'When I walked to Lübeck.'

BACH *scoffs at them*.

BACH. 'The sons cut the father down to size.'

CARL. If we could cut you down to size you wouldn't be so fat.

BACH. Can't you step outside the cliché?

WILHELM. Well can't you tell a different story?

BACH. No.

Thoughtfully –

The River Trave runs round Lübeck. I brought back some shells with me...

BARBARA.... You gave them to me when we got married.

They exchange a fond look. Meanwhile CARL *has been flicking through the cello suites, bursts out laughing.*

CARL. Bloody hell. This gigue is so chromatic and crazy, there's no *way* you could dance to it. (*Laughs.*) Only *you* could work a sexy French wiggle into something so German and angsty and tortured. Hilarious.

(*To the others, generally.*) He's relentless! No wonder he's fat. He eats up the Italians, then moves on to the French. He gobbles up the violin, then he conquers the cello –

BACH. You're wrong. You *can* dance to it. You can dance to all of them. I bet you I can.

CARL. Go on, then!

CARL *begins to play snatches of the cello suites.* BACH *starts to demonstrate dance steps, to the family's amusement.*

BACH. Sarabande. Bourrée. Gavotte.

Everything is a dance.

Life is a dance.

Come on. I can't dance on my own. Wilhelm, come here and dance.

BACH *starts to whirl* WILHELM *round in a dance.*

Listen to this. Can you hear the cello?

The cello rises above CARL*'s harpsichord playing as* BACH *dances with* WILHELM. CARL *slowly stands from the harpsichord and watches his father dance with* WILHELM, *as does* BARBARA.

WILHELM *submits for a while, then becomes claustrophobic, and roughly detaches himself.*

WILHELM. Oh, get *off*, Dad.

Get off!!

BACH *stops. The music fades.*

BARBARA. Dance with *me*, darling.

Pause. BACH *is breathless, shakes his head.*

BACH. I'm out of puff.

Beat.

BARBARA (*quietly*). When was the last time you danced with me?

BACH (*curtly*). I said, I'm out of puff.

The BOYS *silently register this clash. Pause.*

BARBARA. Daddy's right, you know. You can say anything you want with music. You can ask a question. Or you can give an answer.

Beat.

Like your slow movement in the Double Violin Concerto.

She sings it briefly. Then –

(*Bitterly.*) <u>Yearning.</u>

It's as plain as the nose on your face.

…I'm going to go and check on the baby.

She goes out. WILHELM *looks up at the tree.*

WILHELM. My candle is still going strong.

WILHELM *takes* GOTTFRIED *by the hand.*

Which one is yours, Gottfried?

GOTTFRIED *points at a candle.*

Silly. That one's already gone out.

My one is that one up there.

CARL *turns to* BACH.

CARL. Why are you so horrible to Mum?

BACH. What are you talking about?

CARL. Why wouldn't you dance with her?

BACH. For God's sake.

I wasn't in the mood.

CARL. Why not make the effort for her?

BACH. Because it would be a lie.

Beat. WILHELM *takes* GOTTFRIED*'s hand again.*

WILHELM. I'm going to go and help them with the baby.

CARL. Yes, that's right. Don't stick your neck out.

WILHELM *and* GOTTFRIED *walk out. Silence.*

We lie to you all the time, you know. To spare your feelings.

BACH. You could have fooled me.

Pause.

Carl, it's not black and white.

CARL. Most other things seem to be.

BACH. No. It's possible to love someone and be irritated by them at the same time.

CARL. Yes. But the proportions are all wrong.

It's dissonant.

Silence. KATHARINA *comes in. She is upset. She goes to get some towels.*

BACH. Is everything all right?

KATHARINA *shakes her head.*

KATHARINA. I need the little towels. And the big china bowl.

CARL. What's wrong?

KATHARINA. The baby. I tried giving him a cool bath but he's burning up.

BACH. You mean he's got a fever?

KATHARINA. Yes.

BACH. Where is he?

KATHARINA. I left him with Barbara. I've kept him naked to try and bring it down.

I don't know what to do…

CARL. Don't worry.

KATHARINA *is near tears*.

KATHARINA. But it's my fault.

CARL. Why?

KATHARINA. I had it first and I gave it to Gottfried. It was a cough, I had a cough. Gottfried caught it off me. And now the baby has it.

She tries to contain tears.

He is so little and he's gone a funny blue colour.

There is a nonplussed pause.

BACH (*to* CARL). Go and help your mother.

CARL *leaves*.

KATHARINA *now finally allows herself to cry*. BACH *is awkward, and does not know what to do*.

BACH. …It's all right. Katharina.

Beat.

Katharina. It will be all right. Don't cry.

He pats her arm.

KATHARINA. It's all my fault.

BACH. It's not your fault.

KATHARINA. It is.

BACH. Nonsense.

KATHARINA. It's punishment for my feelings.

BACH *looks at her, totally baffled*.

BACH. What feelings?

Crying, KATHARINA *buries her head into his chest*.

KATHARINA. My feelings.

BACH *stands there, woodenly, while she weeps on him. Then, carefully, gently, he detaches himself. He walks out.*

KATHARINA *tries to gather herself.*

She looks up at the tree. All the candles have now gone out, except for one.

She looks up at it. It is guttering. Suddenly the room is very dark. She focuses on the candle, willing it to stay alight. Music: Cello Suite No. 5 in C minor – Prelude. Slowly, she crosses herself.

As she gazes at it, the candle suddenly burns brighter, then slowly goes out.

Scene Six

BARBARA *lies propped up in bed, ill, asleep.*

KATHARINA *busies herself about the room, quietly replenishing a bowl of water. She stirs the fire. Feels* BARBARA*'s forehead.*

CARL *comes to the door of the room.*

CARL. Is she any better?

> KATHARINA *doesn't answer, puts her finger to her lips. Then –*

KATHARINA (*whispers*). Can you go and get some more hot water and some clean cloths. And the chamomile I made her please.

CARL. Yes.

> *He turns to go, then –*

Why the hell isn't he here?

KATHARINA *frowns.*

KATHARINA. Sh.

> CARL *leaves.* BARBARA *stirs, wakes up. She tries to get out of bed.* KATHARINA *restrains her.*

KATHARINA. No, sweetheart. Stay there. You're not well.

BARBARA. I need to get up.

KATHARINA. You don't. We need to get you better, first.

> *Pause.*

BARBARA. Where's the baby.

> *Beat.*

KATHARINA. The baby died, darling.

BARBARA. Oh, that's right.

> *Pause. She listens.*

It's so windy out.

KATHARINA. Yes.

> *Pause.* BARBARA *starts to try to get out of bed again.* KATHARINA *puts her hand on her.*

Don't, darling. What is it. I'll get it for you.

BARBARA (*struggling weakly*). I want to go outside.

KATHARINA. Outside? What for?

BARBARA. I'm worried about the baby.

KATHARINA. What do you mean?

> *Beat.*

BARBARA. I wish we hadn't buried him under the pear tree.

It's windy... he'll be cold out there... the wind will scare him.

KATHARINA. Barbara –

> *But* BARBARA *has managed to get out of bed.*

BARBARA. I went out before. When you weren't here. To check on him.

KATHARINA. For goodness' sake.

BARBARA. I put a blanket down on the ground to keep him warm. But now it will have blown away.

Beat.

KATHARINA. The pear tree will shelter him.

BARBARA. No it won't. All the blossoms have blown off.

Beat.

Poor Katharina. You look so worried. Try not to worry so much.

CARL *comes in with water and chamomile, followed by* WILHELM.

WILHELM. Mummy, what are you doing? Get back in bed.

BARBARA. If it makes you happy.

WILHELM. Tea, please.

She wearily sits back down on the bed. Pause.

BARBARA. Where is he?

WILHELM. Who?

BARBARA. Daddy.

CARL. Karlsbad, Mummy. The spa. With Prince Leopold.

BARBARA. Why?

KATHARINA. He doesn't know you're ill, darling.

BARBARA. Oh.

Pause.

(*To her sons.*) Don't be cross with him, please.

She lies back on the bed. WILHELM *takes her hand.*

(*To* WILHELM, *confidentially.*) The one I worry about is Wilhelm. It's like Daddy. He can't get on with people.

WILHELM.... Mummy, I'm Wilhelm.

BARBARA. Oh, yes, that's right. You are. I thought you were Carl.

It's a canon.

Well, I worry about you.

KATHARINA (*in an undertone*). Can you both go. And get Gottfried.

WILHELM. Mummy, we'll be back in a minute.

He goes with CARL.

BARBARA. Who's that playing?

KATHARINA. Gottfried. Practising.

Pause.

BARBARA. He's getting quite good.

Beat.

Music is a conversation. It has complicated moments and simple.

Suddenly she looks directly at KATHARINA.

(*With conviction.*) Please stay and look after the children.

Pause.

KATHARINA (*with great bitterness*). Why do you put up with it?

BARBARA. Because I love him, the stupid bugger.

Beat.

He should marry you, but I don't think he will. He'll marry her.

KATHARINA. What?

BARBARA. He'll marry her. The soprano.

But it won't make him happy.

KATHARINA. What are you talking about, my pet?

BARBARA. Exactly that.

Pause.

Because he loves her.

Nothing has happened. It's not physical. But it doesn't mean it's not real.

Music is sad. But the strings aren't crying. No one is being stabbed. There's no blood. But it's real. Isn't it?

Beat. She studies her. Then –

Oh, poor Katharina. I didn't realise.

The music stops. Whispering from off. Pause.

The BOYS *come in and stand in a line, looking at* BARBARA. *She looks back at them. Music – 'Welt, gute Nacht'.*

Scene Seven

WILHELM *is playing on the harpsichord while* CARL *packs a suitcase.*

CARL (*irritably*). For God's sake, can't you pack?

WILHELM. No. I don't feel like it.

CARL *grumpily puts things into his suitcase. Manuscripts, clothes, books. He walks over to* WILHELM, *listens. Sniffs the air.*

CARL. My God, you're drunk again.

WILHELM. So what. What does it matter.

CARL. Why do you do it?

WILHELM. It helps me feel happy and relaxed.

CARL. Can't you feel happy and relaxed without it?

WILHELM. Are you kidding? Look at yourself. I've never seen anyone more tense.

He plays some more.

CARL. You're so annoying. That's actually good. Did you
write it?

WILHELM. Yes.

CARL. Write it down?

WILHELM. No.

CARL. Why not?

WILHELM. What's the point?

CARL. What do you mean, what's the point?

WILHELM. It's not as good as him, so what's the point?

*He breaks into a super-quick rendition of the Toccata and
Fugue in D minor, taking the mickey out of it, and himself.
Stops with a discordant crash.*

CARL. If you're shit, then what am I?

WILHELM. You're fucking ruthless. That's what you are.

CARL. You… *virtuoso*.

WILHELM. Creep.

CARL. *Improviser.*

WILHELM *half-heartedly plays a few more notes.*

WILHELM. Listen to the way he's tuned it. All the major thirds
are sharper than pure.

CARL. It's his own special tuning. It means he can play in all
the keys. Wander into different keys without you realising.

WILHELM. Have you noticed, he writes a lot of pieces about
death in G major?

CARL. Well. He likes breaking the rules.

WILHELM. He's so good at misery.

WILHELM *gets up, looks in* CARL*'s bag.*

He picks up some notebooks.

What do you write in all of these?

CARL. Notes. To help me remember stuff.

WILHELM. Bloody hell. What's this?

He lifts up some little bags of money.

CARL. Can you stop *touching* everything? It's my savings.

WILHELM. From what?

CARL. Teaching the Freiburgs harpsichord.

WILHELM (*grudging admiration*). You're a machine.

CARL. No. I just don't ever want to be poor.

WILHELM *lies down on the floor.*

WILHELM. Why do we have to move to *Leipzig*, anyway?

CARL. Because he keeps cocking up and quarrelling and falling out with people. He's completely hopeless.

WILHELM. Makes a change.

CARL (*an explanation*), Prince Leopold got married. And his new wife doesn't like Dad's stuff. So now Dad's out.

WILHELM. Why doesn't she like it?

CARL. Well, it's hardly what you'd call fashionable.

WILHELM. I couldn't be fashionable even if I knew how, and I don't.

CARL. You know, it gets very wearing, you being the genius all the time.

WILHELM. Why don't you try composing, then?

CARL. I can't.

I'm ashamed.

WILHELM. Then that makes two of us.

Beat.

I want to write something that's like perfume, rising.

CARL. Oh. You mean strings.

Pause. CARL *continues to pack.*

Opera's how to make your name, anyway.

WILHELM. How do you know?

CARL. Everyone knows that.

Pause.

Leipzig'll be an upgrade for Dad. Of sorts. As Kappellmeister he'll get four town pipers, three violinists and one apprentice.

Beat.

He makes out he's so unworldly but it's just pathetic what he cares about. How much free beer he gets with the job, he haggled for ages about that. And that he's referred to as Kappellmeister not Kantor, I mean he really gives a shit. So he's Kappellmeister and we're going to go to the Thomasschule. Then, we're to study Law at Leipzig.

WILHELM. Law??!

CARL. Yes. So we've got a profession.

WILHELM. How depressing.

CARL. He's got it all worked out.

Beat.

I think you should have a shave.

WILHELM *groggily gets up.*

WILHELM. How come you *know* all this?

CARL. You should try not being drunk for a change. And eavesdropping instead. It's very informative.

WILHELM *goes over to the mirror, splashes water on his face from a bowl.*

WILHELM. What about those concertos he wrote for Brandenburg? Didn't that come to anything?

CARL *laughs bitterly.*

CARL. Six concertos and the bastard didn't even write back. You know Dad copied it all out himself, wouldn't trust a copyist? Can you imagine how long it took him? That's what I mean. He's completely hopeless. Tone deaf when it comes to sycophancy.

WILHELM. To be fair, he was using up old material.

CARL. Nothing wrong with that.

Beat.

WILHELM. Mummy would be happy that he's going back to a church. She hated him working at court.

CARL. She always wanted him to write his Passion. Now maybe he will.

CARL comes and looks over WILHELM's shoulder in the mirror.

You've missed a bit.

WILHELM shaves it. Stops, and looks at CARL in the mirror.

WILHELM, How funny.., your face isn't like that in real life. It's completely the other way round.

He turns to look at CARL's actual face.

Did you know Maria Freiburg fancies you?

CARL. Yes, I did know. I'm not interested.

WILHELM. Why not? I would be.

CARL. Because I'm more interested in music, at the moment.

WILHELM. Why?

CARL. Because music is sex *and* maths *and* drama *and* sculpture.

WILHELM. Sometimes.

CARL moves away, continues packing.

You know what Dad said to me once? He said women are delicious. I said, What, like fried potatoes are delicious? And he said Yes, exactly like fried potatoes.

He pauses, and then, suddenly, his eyes fill with tears.

Mummy's uncle wrote 'Welt, gute Nacht'.

CARL. I know. So?

WILHELM. I wish we'd used it at her funeral.

He weeps, silently.

CARL *turns around, notices.*

He goes over and hugs him tenderly.

CARL. Willy. Willy, Willy, Willy. Mum wanted you to be happy.

WILHELM. I know.

CARL. Try to do what she wanted.

WILHELM *sobs.*

WILHELM. I can't… I can't be happy.

CARL. You can.

I'll look after you.

WILHELM. But you're younger than me.

CARL. Doesn't matter.

BACH *comes in.* WILHELM *hastily hides his tears.*

BACH. Have you finished packing yet? I need one of you to help me with the harpsichords.

The BOYS *part.*

CARL. I can help. What do you want done?

BACH. I'm not sure. We probably need to wrap them in blankets first.

CARL (*curiously*). What are you working on? I could hear you all last night.

BACH (*abstractedly*). Erm. A Magnificat. To mark my arrival there. Trouble is, I want the three highest voices to sing in unison with two oboes and I think I only get one oboe there.

CARL. A trumpet would sound the same as two oboes.

BACH (*looking around for something to sit on*)....But I'd have to change the key.

Listen, boys, I've got something to tell you.

He looks around again, abstractedly.

Why the hell isn't there anything to sit on?

CARL. Because we packed it all.

BACH. I see. Thank you.

They look at him.

Anna is coming with us to Leipzig.

WILHELM....Who's Anna?

BACH. The soprano. You met her when we were rehearsing.

Beat.

CARL (*baffled*). Why is Anna coming to Leipzig?

BACH. We're getting married.

WILHELM. What?

CARL. What are you talking about?

Pause.

Mummy died eighteen months ago.

BACH. That's right.

CARL. It's disgusting.

BACH. Carl, that's enough.

Pause.

WILHELM. Does Katharina know?

BACH. Yes.

Beat.

CARL. Have you any idea how upset Mummy would be?

BACH. Mummy is dead.

Beat.

Actually, she wouldn't be upset. She would understand.

And she would try not to mind. Because she would know it was for the best.

CARL. What about your God?

BACH. God understands. We are all poor sinners.

CARL. That's very convenient.

Beat.

I don't think you even miss Mummy.

BACH. Of course I do.

CARL. No, you don't. How could you marry again if you did?

BACH. I'm marrying again *because* I miss Mum.

Beat.

CARL. What did you do, play her your Toccata and Fugue in the organ loft? You make me want to vomit.

BACH *slaps him across the face*.

WILHELM. Dad, don't –

Pause.

BACH. Anna is a kind girl. And she's very talented.

CARL *manages to speak, shaken*.

CARL. Talent, talent, talent – so what? What's so great about talent? If talent is a gift that you're born with, a gift from God, if it doesn't come from being kind, or working hard, or trying your best, then what is talent worth? Nothing.

Pause.

I tell you what, if you marry her, you *will* miss Mum.

Beat.

What did she do, flatter you into falling for her? Sit copying out your music for hours on end, telling you you're a great man? You're not a great man. You might be a great musician but you're a horrible human being –

WILHELM. Carl, stop –

BACH. This is a tantrum. Stop behaving like a spoilt child.

CARL. You're the spoilt child. Mum spoilt you. And you couldn't even be on time for her death! You missed it. *You were six weeks late.*

Now it is as if CARL *has slapped* BACH *– he flinches.*

WILHELM *starts to weep again.*

WILHELM. Carl. He didn't know.

CARL. If he'd come back when he said he would, he would have been on time. She held on as long as she could.

Beat.

It's not for God that we all suffer. We suffer for *you*, because *you* want to live forever. Well, I'm not a believer any more. You eat everything alive and you bully and you're exhausting and relentless. But you'll die too in the end.

Beat.

BACH. Have you finished?

CARL. No.

Why weren't you nicer to Mummy when she was alive?

Beat.

BACH. Have it your own way. You're right. Talent can't be willed, or worked for. And neither can love.

ANNA *comes in, watches, silently.*

You don't get love for trying hard, or being kind, or working hard. Love isn't fair, either.

He walks out. ANNA *stays, watching.*

CARL *weeps*.

WILHELM *hugs him*.

The Magnificat plays, triumphantly.

ANNA *sings the Magnificat.*

Blackout.

End of Act One.

ACT TWO

Scene One

CARL *sits at a harpsichord, dressed in court finery, accompanying* FREDERICK THE GREAT, *who stands playing the flute. They reach the end of the piece. Pause.*

FREDERICK....So. What did you think?

Beat.

CARL. It was wonderful, Majesty.

FREDERICK. Yes?

CARL. Yes. Accomplished, serene. Your Majesty shows great prowess as a composer.

FREDERICK. It lacks something. It sounds oddly flat – as if it's only one melody, one voice.

CARL. Not at all.

FREDERICK. No? Are you sure?

CARL. Quite sure.

FREDERICK. Oh come off it.

It is though, really, isn't it. One voice, Even though there are two instruments.

CARL. Not at all. It is rich and layered.

FREDERICK. No. They sing as one. And one melody is not really a conversation.

Is it.

Beat.

CARL....Majesty?

FREDERICK. Unison is nice. But two voices can't continue in the same direction forever. They need to diverge if the melody is to be interesting.

Beat. He is amused by CARL's *confusion and discomfort.*

I do like a *little* bit of honesty. It gives flavour – like salt.

Beat.

CARL (*warily, uncertainly*). The... lack is all on my side, Majesty. I must practise my part. (*Shuffles together the score.*)

FREDERICK (*coldly*). Yes. Well. Have it your own way. We've got a couple of days before the concert. I don't get nervous any more, which is good.

He puts down the flute, stretches, looks at CARL *curiously.*

I've heard all about you, you know. That's why you were offered the appointment.

CARL *bows.*

A student at Leipzig who is writing thirty sonatas. Your keyboard concertos. That one in A minor. Let's have a bit of that. Go on.

CARL *sits again at the harpsichord, plays with brio the Allegro Assai from the Keyboard Concerto in A minor.* FREDERICK *interrupts him.*

Yes. It's so interesting. How dramatic it is. And yet you are such a very crushed young person. Where does all that passion come from?

CARL *doesn't answer.*

I hope you'll enjoy yourself here. You'll only be required to play every other week. I have other tutors and accompanists, old faithfuls, like Quantz, for instance, my flute teacher, or Benda, he's the concertmaster. Paid better than you, more privileges than you. They are your superiors. Which is funny, given that you're the most talented. But that's what I decided. I could change my mind, of course.

Until then, you'll have plenty of time to amuse yourself here. Berlin is *very* amusing.

Have you seen this?

He walks over to a mechanical cockerel. Presses a lever. The cockerel sings a mechanical crowing song.

I love mechanical music.

CARL. Extraordinary.

FREDERICK. Not extraordinary. But amusing. The first time, at least.

It's all to do with valves. Mechanical vibrations passing throughout the different chambers within.

Beat.

I'm thinking of buying a few Klaviers, as well. These new fortepianos. They sound fun.

CARL. Indeed.

FREDERICK. What do you think? Shall I?

CARL. Certainly, if Your Majesty –

FREDERICK. I can do that, now my father's dead. I can do anything I want.

It's a wonderful feeling.

My father *really* disapproved of music. He thought it was effeminate.

Beat.

What do you think? Is music effeminate?

CARL. …I couldn't presume to say.

FREDERICK. I practise for four hours a day. The flute goes everywhere with me. That probably makes me *very* effeminate. But I find it a comfort. Isn't music a comfort? Isn't that what it's for? – I also have a travelling harpsichord. It's collapsible.

Beat.

How is *your* father?

CARL. …Your Majesty?

FREDERICK. Yes. How is he?

CARL....I haven't seen my father for some time.

FREDERICK. How much time?

CARL. Years.

Beat.

I think he's well.

FREDERICK. What does your father think music is for?

CARL. I'm not sure.

Beat.

To teach... to persuade... to heal.

FREDERICK. Heal what?

Beat.

My father found me hiding once, reading a book in a bush, when I should have been out hunting.

CARL. What happened?

FREDERICK. At last! A genuine, spontaneous question! A conversation!

Beat.

He gave me the fiercest beating of my life. Oh dear, oh dear. He didn't like me at all. He started beating me regularly when I turned twelve. Exactly the same time I started going through puberty. He hated the fact I curled my hair. He hated me playing the flute. And he hated my best friend, Hans.

It's such a relief that he's dead.

Ah, well. We must all murder our fathers. Not literally, of course.

Well – sometimes.

CARL....But your father did not think that you intended to *murder* him, I am sure?

FREDERICK. Oh no! You're wrong. Wrong. No, he *always* thought I intended to murder him!

He was extremely paranoid. But I didn't need to murder him, in the end. He obliged me with his death.

Beat.

Your father has strong musical opinions, am I right?

CARL. He is a little old-fashioned.

FREDERICK. Likes his counterpoint?

CARL. Indeed.

FREDERICK. His music smells of the church... he would say that music is a code to be solved.

And I would say that we speak in codes. Codes to be solved.

Beat.

I asked that we meet each other alone today. I wanted a solo from you. As it were. But I don't think you've given me one.

CARL....My humblest apologies, Your Majesty.

FREDERICK. There you go again.

Pause.

Once upon a time I tried to run away from my father. I tried to escape with my dear friend Hans.

Beat.

My father found out and had me thrown in prison. Really, he wanted to have me killed, but unfortunately I'm his heir. At five in the morning I was led to the window of my cell and told to watch. On the orders of my father they took my friend Hans out into the courtyard and beheaded him in front of me.

Beat.

The funny thing is, the King thought he took my Hans away from me.

But I feel him here. Near me.

He stares at CARL.

Slowly, FREDERICK *stretches out his hand towards* CARL. *He touches* CARL'*s face, gently.*

I feel him all the time.

Then, he lets his hand fall.

CARL. How cruel.

FREDERICK. Well, I'm his son. I'm his possession, aren't I. To treat badly.

CARL. That's not love.

FREDERICK. It's a variation of it. A variation on a theme.

Beat.

Play me something else.

Slowly, CARL *goes to a cello. He sits, takes it between his legs, begins to play Air on the G String.*

FREDERICK *listens.*

Elsewhere on the stage, BACH *joins, and thoughtfully starts to play the accompaniment on a pianoforte, testing it out.*

Slowly, silently, FREDERICK *begins to cry.*

CARL *looks up at him, hesitantly.*

CARL. Your Majesty?

FREDERICK. Yes?

CARL. Shall I continue?

FREDERICK. Of course.

Beat. He indicates his tears.

These? A mechanical response. To do with the vibrations of the noise itself. Caused by gases in the hollows of the brain which serve to enlarge and contract the chambers of the heart.

Descartes says our feelings number only six. Wonder, love, hate, desire, delight, and sadness.

I'm not sure I have even that many.

(*To himself.*) They have cut deeply into the marble. And that stays forever.

CARL *continues to play, and* FREDERICK *listens, moved despite himself.*

FREDERICK.... Who wrote this?

Beat.

Did you write this?

CARL (*continuing to play*). No.

Beat.

My father did.

He continues to play, and FREDERICK *to listen.*

Scene Two

Late at night. BACH *sits at his desk, composing.*

ANNA *tiptoes in, dressed in her nightie.*

It should feel like an echo of the first scene that we saw between BARBARA *and* BACH.

ANNA *watches* BACH *for a few seconds.*

ANNA. Bastian.

Pause.

What are you writing?

BACH. Seeing as my Passion went down like a turd in a tureen... I thought I'd give it another go.

This is according to St Matthew.

Pause.

Why are you up?

ANNA. I came to get some water for the baby and I saw your light.

Beat. She gestures to her breasts.

He's going to want to eat but I don't have any milk.

I'm a lousy cow.

BACH (*absent-mindedly*). Don't fret.

She comes and looks over his shoulder. BACH *half-heartedly attempts to shield it.*

ANNA. Oh for goodness' sake. Sweetie, you *must* stop going straight to the top about every little thing.

BACH. My salary is not a little thing.

ANNA. The Elector of Saxony doesn't care that you're being paid six florins rather than twelve. It's so petty.

BACH. I've always thought pettiness was a noble emotion. Getting your own squawky little point of view across. It's very important.

ANNA. The more you write to him the less he'll listen.

BACH. I work my arse off for them! A cantata every Sunday and the second it's over I have to sit down and start writing another... it's relentless... they will have had three cycles out of me by Easter –

ANNA (*sharply*). I know, I copy them out for you.

BACH. I wouldn't mind, but they're *shit singers*. I can't even write them an opening chorus, they couldn't cope with learning it for Sunday –

ANNA. But you write for singers as if they're instruments –

BACH. They *should be* instruments. If they're any good.

She glares at him.

It's a compliment. You are, my darling.

ANNA. Maybe if you *taught* them, like you're supposed to, they would get better.

BACH. No. I've had enough. I wrote to the council today telling them which ones are the worst. I want all the duds replaced. All seventeen of them.

ANNA. Bastian! You didn't *name* them, did you?

BACH. Of course I did.

ANNA. Oh God.

BACH. And I need at least eleven more instrumentalists.

He gestures at his score.

Otherwise, there's really no point in me writing all this, because no one will be able to play it. And if they won't give them to me, they can't complain if I go elsewhere.

ANNA. What do you mean?

BACH. The Collegium Musicum. Proper musicians. I can do both jobs.

ANNA. You can't. You're working flat out already. The council will fire you.

BACH (*imperviously, musing*). It would be different if I could do more *funerals*... that would bring in a few bob... but these Leipzigers, they just won't fucking *die*... (*Brightly.*) Of course, there are the hymns before the *hangings*, but –

ANNA. Darling. Listen to me. Stop it for a second. We don't *need* more money.

BACH. In case you hadn't noticed, I have a lot of children to support.

ANNA. But the little ones don't cost anything.

BACH. I'm talking about the big ones. I'm bailing out sons left, right and centre...

ANNA. Well stop! You should stop! Stop giving Wilhelm money, stop giving Gottfried money, let them screw their lives up themselves.

BACH. Wilhelm needs my support.

ANNA. He is a grown man.

BACH. He's fragile.

ANNA. He's a drunk.

BACH. He *drinks*, and he's talented.

ANNA. When he went for the job at Dresden, you wrote the
letter of recommendation, you copied out the piece for his
audition, you filled out the application for him, and you
signed his name for him. You *make* him fragile. *Gottfried* –

BACH. Gottfried –

ANNA. – runs up debts in every job you get him. Step back.
Let them fail, let them be free, it's what they want, it's the
only way they'll learn.

BACH *sighs heavily.*

BACH. Gottfried… I don't understand. He hasn't even got a
family, only got his cock to care for. Where's all the money
going? He was obsessive, a perfectionist when he was three.
Hours with his blocks. 'Making a long bridge, Daddy.' What
happened to all that discipline?

ANNA. People change.

…You make favourites of them and it damages them.

BACH. I have to look after them. They lost their mother.

ANNA. But *I* was here.

Pause.

Why don't you ever help Carl?

Carl lost his mother, too.

BACH. Carl doesn't need my help.

ANNA. Maybe that's because you don't help him all the time.

Pause.

BACH (*with weariness*). Life is a mess.

Willy has such talent, but he has no… application.

It pains me to look at him. He's getting older, fatter…

Pause.

He's more talented than Carl but he will fail.

ANNA. There is nothing you can do for him.

BACH. He will fail. Like me.

Beat.

ANNA. You see yourself in him. But there's a big difference. You have enormous application. He doesn't.

BACH. But why?

ANNA. I don't know. Why does the sun rise and the moon set. I don't know why you get into petty arguments with people all the time. Picking fights with that horrible Scheibe. Darling. I thought you were a happy person. You were when we met. Now, you're constantly rowing, cross, nothing's right, it's like you're unhappy in your own skin…

BACH. I think it's called getting older.

ANNA. No. It's just like Mühlhausen, it's like Köthen, it's the same cycle over and over again. Alienating the council, shoving librettists around, silly quarrels – this obsessive stuff, this streak, is great for writing ten-line fugues, not so much for life. You're like a harpsichord. Even when you want to play gently –

She demonstrates.

– or hard –

She demonstrates, with a thump – the harpsichord rings out, unchanged –

It comes out at exactly the same volume, because you can't modify yourself –

BACH. I don't want to modify myself!! Why should I? Scheibe said I was turgid, unnatural and overwritten. To which I say, I taught him for a year and I always hated his slippers. Do you remember his slippers? It's all because I didn't give him that post as my organist. He's a bitter shit. Scheibe by name, Scheisse by nature –

ANNA. But why do you *care* so much what Scheibe prints about you? He's a mediocrity. A flea. Don't scratch.

There is a sudden silence.

BACH. ...It hurts my sense of order.

I know he's wrong. It's not about conceit. I hate a lie.

I looked at my old scores tonight. I'm running out of time. I wanted to keep them for all my children.

But what's the point?

Beat.

I want to believe in order more than ever. But all the evidence points the other way.

There's no order or logic to anything.

ANNA. Do you still have faith?

BACH. ...I have doubt. It feels like the same thing. A version of it.

ANNA (*quietly*). Yes. You're right. Doubt.

Pause.

We started so well. The notebook you made me, songs for me to sing. Emerald silk binding, tied with a tasselled ribbon.

Christiana, Heinrich, Christian, Liesgen. Four in four years.

Beat.

Christiana died on this day.

BACH. ...I know.

ANNA. Three years old.

Beat.

She was my favourite because she was our first. Is it wrong that she was my favourite? Is that why he took her away from us?

BACH *silently shakes his head.*

I wish we hadn't got to know her. I explained it to myself –
she had to make space in the world for Liesgen. Do you
remember how Liesgen loved eating earth?

But then, Ernestus? Why? Immediately. Before we even
washed him.

BACH. Because he wasn't fit for this world. It was a blessing.

ANNA. Christian?

BACH. God's will.

*ANNA has started to walk around the room, tapping surfaces
rhythmically, rubbing her fingers and thumbs together.*

Christiana Benedicta. Such a fat baby.

BACH (*warily*). Legs like a sofa.

ANNA. I thought all that fat would protect her. Now I feel sick
every year when I see the trees starting to lose their leaves.
Because she was born in the spring, made it through
summer, the winter killed her.

BACH. ... You're tapping again.

ANNA. Because it might keep them safe. If I can just tap the
right time.

BACH. You know it's superstition.

ANNA. But so is everything, perhaps.

*Looking at him meaningfully, she bitterly, ironically crosses
herself. Then continues to tap.*

Christiana Dorothea. Lived for one year. Got a funny rash
that started round her mouth, spread all over her body and
down her legs, died. We kept calling them Christiana after
the last one that died. And they kept dying.

Five little ones. Dead.

BACH. We have four healthy children. Heinrich, Liesgen,
Regina, and little Johann.

ANNA. Heinrich will never be quite right. Not after that labour.

And now Regina has a fever.

Weary now, she stops tapping.

I can't remember not being pregnant, burying children. Am I being punished?

BACH. What for, my love?

ANNA. Because I stole you.

Pause.

I think you grieved your first children more.

BACH. Not true. Each one is different. I grieve each one differently.

Beat.

And you're wrong. It wasn't Liesgen who loved eating earth.

It was Christian.

Pause. ANNA *turns to go. Then she turns back.*

ANNA. You were talking in your sleep again tonight.

BACH. What was I saying?

ANNA. I couldn't understand.

And then I woke up, and you had gone.

On an impulse, she goes over, leafs through the scores. Picks up the one that stands on the harpsichord. Reads it, silently.

Slowly, we hear the opening notes of the Chaconne.

When did you write this?

BACH. I can't remember. It's a Chaconne. Ten years ago. Another time.

ANNA *keeps reading the score and the music continues.* BARBARA *appears in the shadows, only her face is lit.*

ANNA....Oh, Bastian.

She looks at him, sadly.

Do you miss her so much?

BACH *does not answer. The music continues to play.* ANNA *looks back at the score.*

One violin but the sound of two. A violin and its ghost. Using double stops, playing two strings at once, bringing her back to life.

The music continues to play. Pause. Then –

BACH....I have this dream. She's alive but a long way away from me. Her face glows but it's fading. I blow on it to keep the fire alive...

He blows, very gently, in the direction of BARBARA, *who simply stands, watching – her face glows brighter as he blows –*

And it glows brighter and then it fades away.

The light dims on BARBARA's *face, dimmer than before. She retreats a step, into the shadows. But* BACH *moves towards her. Then he begins, slowly, to dance with her.*

ANNA *watches, sadly. The Chaconne plays on as* BACH *and* BARBARA *dance.*

Scene Three

CARL *stands with* WILHELM. CARL *is leafing through one of the many scores piled up on and around the harpsichord.* CARL *is dressed in expensive clothes.* WILHELM *is shabby. As the scene proceeds,* WILHELM *steadily pours himself drinks from a bottle. At the beginning of the scene, he is not drunk.*

CARL. Bloody hell.

WILHELM. Yes.

Beat.

It didn't go down very well. He did it to make a splash.

In a way, it was his opera.

It didn't work.

CARL. He just wants it all, doesn't he?

He scans.

Every key. Old greedyguts.

He carries on looking at the score.

And *that's* just a torturous weird figure. Totally unhelpful, slippy, upsetting.

WILHELM. It's meant to be. It's a crowd not knowing where to go.

The crowd don't come out of it all that brilliantly. They did crucify him I suppose.

CARL. It just makes me feel anxious. The key's got completely lost.

He carries on reading. Turns a page.

Wow. Then he's like, Oh let's invert it!

And these laborious oboes…

Bass is there but not quite working…

He's hitting every tone in the scale before the choir even comes *in*.

...I suppose it represents God quite well.

WILHELM. Or anguish.

CARL....He annoys the fuck out of me, but he is brilliant.

He looks at his pocket watch.

He's late. As usual. Can't believe it... I've come all the way from Berlin, and *I* can be on time...

He looks at WILHELM.

How are you?

WILHELM (*gruffly*). Fine.

CARL. How's Dresden?

WILHELM. Fine.

CARL. How much longer are you going to stay there?

WILHELM. Do I need to move? I'm not harming anyone, am I?

CARL. I didn't say you were.

Beat.

It's just –

Nothing.

Beat.

So how's Anna?

WILHELM. She's all right. I quite like her now. She's very... human.

Or animal, actually. She's like a bird. She sings when she's happy and she sings when she's sad.

Beat.

They lost Regina in the end. She died when she was five. And baby Johann died the same year.

CARL (*winded*). My God. That makes... seven dead?

WILHELM. Yes.

Pause.

You were right, by the way. The one he really misses now is Mum.

CARL. I don't want to be proved right any more.

Beat.

When will he learn to love the one in front of him?

WILHELM. You know what he's like.

...Restless.

Beat.

CARL. Did he read that score I sent him?

WILHELM. I think so. He's had some trouble with his eyes.

You'll see. He's got older.

CARL. Well of course he has.

WILHELM. No, you'll see what I mean.

Beat.

CARL. So do we know where Gottfried might be?

WILHELM. No idea.

CARL. Dad had to go to Mühlhausen to pay off his debts?

WILHELM. Yeah. And then he disappeared. Vanished.

Pause.

CARL. I'm feeling anxious.

WILHELM. It's probably your shoes. They look too tight.

They both gaze out of the window.

CARL. The apple tree has got blight.

WILHELM. I know. All its fruit grows rotten.

– Anyway. *You* look like you're doing well. You're famous, now.

Beat.

CARL. I'm all right.

WILHELM. What's King Frederick like?

CARL. His attitude to people is the same as hazelnuts. He likes shelling them.

Beat in which he wrestles with himself, then –

Willy, for God's sake, why don't you *leave* Dresden? It's ridiculous. How long have you been the organist there, ten years? It's fine as a first job but you can't make your name pootling on the organ there –

WILHELM. I don't want to make my name.

CARL. And you're too close to Dad. You need to get further away.

WILHELM. I'm happy there.

CARL. You don't look happy. You don't look happy at all.

BACH *comes in.*

Hello.

BACH. Carl.

There is an awkward moment, then they embrace.

CARL. Dad, I'm so sorry about Regina. And little Johann. Wilhelm told me.

BACH. It can't be helped.

Pause.

CARL. What can I do about Gottfried? Do you need money?

BACH. No, I already paid off his debts.

CARL. Anna said you were short of money.

BACH. She had no business saying that.

Beat.

If you could use your influence at court to find out where Gottfried has ended up, that would be helpful.

CARL. Of course. I'll try.

Beat.

Where was he last seen?

BACH. Sangerhausen. I got him a job there after the fiasco at Mühlhausen. He promised me he'd change his ways. Then the Burgomaster wrote to me to say he'd run up enormous debts and disappeared again.

CARL. I'll ask.

BACH. You needn't have come all this way. It was pointless.

CARL. I wanted to see you.

Beat.

Willy says your eyesight is going.

BACH. My eyes are fine.

CARL. Dad, you know there is an open invitation for you to come to court. Any time. Frederick is very keen to meet you.

BACH. Frederick the Great. I don't want to. There's no need.

CARL. Don't be stupid. It's a wonderful opportunity. He's a huge admirer of yours.

BACH. Bollocks. I've done all that stuff before, it didn't get me anywhere. It's a waste of time.

Thanks, anyway.

Beat.

CARL. Dad, I don't understand. You obviously care about your... legacy, I mean, why else do you file all this stuff –

BACH. Stuff? You mean, music?

CARL. Yes. I can see, it's organised. Obsessively. But what's the use if no one knows who you are.

BACH. No one needs to know who I am. This is about family. The music got passed down to me... I added to it... and I will pass it on to you lot. And you will add to it, in your turn.

CARL. But don't you want anyone else to *hear* it?

BACH. How many times do I have to tell you, music is for God. We are not the authors of our success.

CARL. But we can design our own failure.

Pause.

Did you read the score I sent you?

BACH. Yes.

KATHARINA *comes in.*

KATHARINA. Darling duck, they told me you were here.

WILHELM (*suddenly bursts out*). Yes! He's home! He's come back!! We should give a speech! He's come back!

KATHARINA *ignores this, comes straight over and hugs* CARL.

CARL. Katharina. You smell exactly the same. Chicken soup.

KATHARINA. Carl, *really.*

CARL. You know what I mean. (*Gesturing at* BACH.) I'm just trying to get Dad to tell me what he thought of my score.

KATHARINA. Are you hungry? Shall I get you some dumplings? I made them specially.

CARL. Honestly, I'm fine.

She looks around distractedly.

KATHARINA. Has anyone told Anna you're here yet?

CARL. No. Stop fussing.

KATHARINA. Or a bit of bread and cheese.

CARL. No, thanks. (*To* BACH). Well? What did you think?

Beat.

BACH. Of the score?

CARL. Yes! Of the score! Come on, the suspense is unbearable.

Beat.

BACH....It's impressive, yes.

CARL. Yes but?

BACH. 'Yes but'?

CARL. I hear a silent 'but'.

Beat.

Well?

BACH. All right, all right... I'm just trying to work out what I think.

It's got beautiful figures... elegance, panache –

Beat.

But for me, it's... swollen. Empty.

CARL. What do you mean, empty?

BACH. Well. It's just sensual pleasure. Isn't it?

CARL. Oh.

– I thought that's what you liked. Sensual pleasure.

KATHARINA. *Carl.*

WILHELM (*under his breath*). For he's a jolly good fellow...

BACH. It's just... not for me.

CARL. Come on, Dad! Don't do me in with *vagueness*.

BACH. All right. Music without a sense of the divine is... empty. There are mysteries that we can't explain. We don't know. We don't *know* everything. And music can do that. This... your... It *sounds* nice, but what is there to it beyond that?

CARL. Nothing matters in music except how it sounds.

WILHELM (*under his breath*). And so say all of us.

BACH. You sound like Scheibe. It wasn't you, writing under an alias, was it?

KATHARINA. What a horrid thing to say.

CARL. Scheibe might have a point. What matters in music is whether it sounds natural, and beautiful.

BACH. Then you end up with polite entertainment. I want music you need to listen to with your eyes wide open and your brain alive.

CARL. But people don't want this mad mathematical ten-line shit! It's exhausting. They just want a gust of wind, to relax. What's wrong with that? You don't have to be tortured. Just have a coffee in the sun.

KATHARINA. Or maybe broth, to warm you up, with bread and butter.

BACH. For crying out loud, he doesn't want anything to eat!! (*To* CARL). Fine.

Maybe it's just after writing music for forty years I want it to sound like me.

WILHELM. Mm. Just *maybe*?

Beat.

CARL. ...I'll be honest with you, Dad, your music – yes it's impressive, but is it always enjoyable to listen to? Your music can be difficult to love.

BACH. Good. It should be difficult to love. People are difficult to love.

Beat.

CARL. When did you actually read my score?

ANNA *comes in.*

ANNA. Carl, how lovely to see you.

CARL. Anna.

They kiss each other.

You're looking beautiful.

ANNA. What brings you back?

CARL. I thought I had something worth showing Dad.

To BACH, *who is now riffling through piles of scores.*

Dad? When did you actually *read* it? I sent it to you a year ago. And didn't hear anything.

BACH *has found* CARL's *score.*

BACH. Ah. Yes. Here it is.

He leafs through it.

And I'll be honest with you. This sentimental style, this Empfindsamer Stil…

WILHELM (*singing softly*). / The Empfindsamer Stil, oh, the Empfindsamer Stil…

ANNA. / Oh, God, not the Empfindsamer Stil *again*…

BACH…. Yes, that's obviously what you're up to, Carl – and I don't like it.

CARL. What? Why?

BACH. Because there's no discipline to it, as far as I can see. Feelings feelings feelings, prized above all else.

CARL. Why do I feel like I'm ten years old again?

BACH. For a start, why do you all have to *play* in that theatrical way? What are you trying to prove?

CARL. Why do you have to play like you're a lump of wood? What are *you* trying to prove? It's just another affectation.

ANNA. My goodness, it didn't take long, did it –

CARL. You are *allowed* to be emotional when you play. It's not a crime.

BACH. Yes, it is a crime, actually. I can't stand all this… *expressing your feelings.*

CARL. Your Prelude in E minor. Are you telling me that's not expressing feelings?

He impatiently sits at the harpsichord and plays the opening.

It's wonderful. It's *such* a rich, complicated feeling you're voicing, I'm not sure I can put it into words. It's *better* than words – don't tell me your music isn't expressing feelings.

Beat.

BACH (*cornered*). That's not what I said.

My music is expressing feelings.

Just not *my* feelings.

CARL. I don't believe you. I think it's a big fat lie. Your Chaconne for solo violin when Mummy died.

ANNA stiffens, BACH glances protectively at her.

I'm sorry, Anna. But that's what it's about. Sixty-four variations in thirteen minutes. The variety of grief. So much quicker and more precise than words. Why are you so squeamish about admitting to it?

BACH. All right. Because what you lot are doing – I think it's narcissistic. And cynical. Just enough quirks, you package the deal and wrap it up with a bow. A dance, a sad one, a fast one. Keep the harmonic clarity, don't go too far, clear, lucid, a few good textures, some scrubbing on the violins but nothing too shocking. Above all, *efficient*. It leaves me pleading for a little... *raggedness*.

Beat.

CARL. Are you saying that's what my score was doing?

BACH. No, actually, since you ask. This –

He looks at the score again.

There's something altogether more neurotic about it. Something more unwholesome.

CARL. The music? Or me?

BACH. And melodramatic. At times you do a pretty good impression of me.

WILHELM. Dad's right, actually. It's weird. It *is* sort of melodramatic.

CARL (*sourly*). Oh right, you read it too, did you? Great.

WILHELM. No, but I liked it. I really liked it, Carl. I was impressed. Interested. It's all flounce and flair. You've got absolutely no flounce in life. Your nose to the grindstone, taking notes, saving money – all your flounce is in the music. I thought it was great.

CARL. Fuck off.

WILHELM. You *are* him, by the way. Re-entry of the subject in a different voice. The way you mark in all your ornamentation. I got the bit that doesn't get on with people.

CARL (*ignoring this*). Hang on. Let me sort this out. (*To* BACH.) I sent it a *year* ago and I thought you didn't get it. Because I didn't hear anything.

BACH. I did get it.

CARL. So when did you read it?

BACH. A year ago.

CARL. A year ago and you couldn't find time to write and say what you thought?!

BACH. I didn't want to write until I had read it properly.

CARL. 'Properly'?

BACH. Yes, properly.

CARL. So how *did* you read it?

BACH. Five minutes here… five minutes there… I kept getting interrupted.

CARL. … *Wow*. You must have *really* hated it.

BACH. Carl –

CARL. You didn't find time in a year to read it *again*?

BACH (*feebly*). I've been having some trouble with my eyes.

CARL. Unbelievable! You can be cruel without even trying.

CARL *laughs, bitterly.*

BACH. I told you, I wanted to read it properly first!!

KATHARINA *goes to hug* CARL.

KATHARINA. Carl. My little redhead. *I'm* proud of you.

BACH *puts down the score.*

BACH. What are you doing with your life, Carl?

CARL. What?!

BACH. When are you going to get married? That's the most important thing. Why haven't you got married yet? You're too old not to be. When are you going to have children?

KATHARINA. He will in good time.

CARL. What is this? I'm trying to have a career! Is this to do with me being 'unwholesome' or something? (*Re:* WILHELM.) He isn't married either, you know.

BACH. That's not his fault.

CARL. I thought you'd be pleased! That I'd written something. I was pleased with it.

Beat.

Anna wrote you've been bailing Wilhelm out.

ANNA. Carl.

CARL. As well as Gottfried. And that's why you're broke. The unfairness is sort of glorious. They are literally the prodigal sons! What have *they* done? Apart from spend your money? My God, can we just look around ourselves? Who is the penniless drunk in the room? Does one have to be *difficult* to be considered a great artist by you? Do I need to start *cultivating* it? Being a pain in the arse?

BACH. Seems to me you're doing a pretty good job of that already.

CARL (*gestures at* WILHELM). – In case you hadn't noticed, he is obviously drinking himself to death.

WILHELM. I am *here*, you know.

BACH. You're being melodramatic. Like your music.

CARL. The blatant favouritism!

(*To* WILHELM.) How are you not ashamed? To accept his money?

ANNA (*to* BACH). It's true, darling. You're horribly unfair.

CARL. The more hopeless they are, the more you give them your love.

BACH. As does God.

CARL. What about the ones who aren't hopeless? Pretty tough on us lot.

BACH. I give to those who need.

CARL. He's a pisshead!

WILHELM (*to* CARL). It doesn't feel great, taking his money. But it's the same as you wanting him to like your music. I could say, aren't you ashamed to ask him to like your music? But we're both the same. We need him.

KATHARINA. Willy's right. (*Appealing to* BACH.) For goodness' sake. Carl just wants your approval. Can't you give it to him?

BACH. I said, it was impressive!

WILHELM. Bravo! Katharina's got some backbone.

He goes over to CARL.

Don't be upset. If it's any consolation, he doesn't like my music either. Not really.

CARL. Yes. But at least he likes *you*.

He walks out.

ANNA. Go after him, for God's sake.

BACH. There's no point. He needs to cool off.

Beat.

I'm exhausted.

Beat.

ANNA. All he wants is your love.

BACH. Well then he should ask for my love. Not for me to like his music.

ANNA. It's hard to ask for love.

Beat.

BACH. I'm tired.

...I'm going to lie down.

He goes out. ANNA *is upset.*

ANNA. What a mess.

Beat. WILHELM *is suddenly deflated.*

WILHELM. He's not cruel. He's just impatient.

ANNA. It feels the same when you're on the receiving end.

Beat.

I'm going after him.

She goes out. WILHELM *and* KATHARINA *contemplate each other for a moment.*

WILHELM. Poor Katharina. The canon goes round. A one-way circular system.

Beat.

Everyone is unrequitedly in love with him. You, Anna, Carl...

Beat.

KATHARINA. Not unrequitedly. He came to me once. After Barbara died.

I was the closest thing he could find to her.

Only once.

So yes. Unrequited.

They stare at each other.

Music plays – the opening of the St John Passion.

Scene Four

BACH *stands with* WILHELM. *They are in travelling clothes. Moonlight.* BACH *is exhausted.*

Around them, frozen, stand the figures of the court of FREDERICK THE GREAT, *poised, in mid-animation.*

WILHELM. We don't need to. Please.

BACH. No.

WILHELM. Tell them you need to rest. *I'll* tell them.

   BACH *steadies himself.*

BACH. No. We were summoned.

WILHELM. We've been travelling seventy-two hours straight. You need to sleep first. In a bed.

BACH. No. Let's get it over with.

And suddenly, the lights are up on the court scene and BACH *and* WILHELM *stand, blinking, dazzled.* CARL *is just finishing playing a piece of music on the harpsichord to assembled guests. He turns first to see* BACH *and* WILHELM, *crumpled and dishevelled in their travelling gear.* FREDERICK *follows his gaze, holds up his hand, and* CARL *abruptly stops playing.*

FREDERICK (*an announcement*). Gentlemen.

Everyone now swivels to look at BACH *and* WILHELM.

(*A note of triumph in his voice*.) Gentlemen! At last.

Old Bach is here.

FLUNKEYS *move in to relieve* BACH *and* WILHELM *of their coats.*

Meanwhile FREDERICK *eyes* BACH *sharply. Then* –

Are you Old Bach?

BACH. I am.

FREDERICK. Really?

BACH. Yes.

Drinks are proffered. CARL *rises stiffly from the harpsichord, goes uncertainly towards* BACH. *Then, awkwardly, after a false start, he kisses him.* WILHELM *bows.*

CARL (*a greeting*). Father.

– Wilhelm.

FREDERICK *looks at the incomplete family critically.*

FREDERICK. What an honour it is finally to meet you.

Beat.

Oh dear. Did we not give you time to change?

BACH. I must apologise for my appearance, Majesty. No.

FREDERICK. No matter.

He gestures.

May I introduce – your grandchild. Your first, if I am not mistaken?

CARL *ushers forward a small boy, played by the same actor who played the young Gottfried, in court finery. He steps forward to bow before* BACH. BACH *is shocked.*

Yes. You are surprised? Your son has finally got married.

He looks at CARL *wryly.*

Married to a goose – but married.

BACH *stares at the little boy.*

BACH. I am... charmed.

FREDERICK (*carelessly*). I, too, am married to a goose. But I have no children.

He walks towards the CHILD, *who stands uncomfortably rooted to the spot, clearly wishing to make his escape.* FREDERICK *ruffles the* CHILD*'s hair.*

Our children...

They are our crimes, our conscience, our reproach.

That's why I don't want them.

He moves away.

Well, Herr Bach, we have been preparing for your arrival. For days, now.

(*To* WILHELM.) You have something to drink?

Good.

(*To* BACH.) To eat? Good.

He gestures around him.

Here, you see, the new keyboards. Bought specially. The very latest to be designed.

They have the ability, for the first time ever, to have their volume controlled.

He demonstrates, playing a few notes –

I can increase it – and decrease it. Just as I choose.

With a flourish –

This – is known as the new *fortepiano.*

BACH *inspects the instrument, grimly.* CARL *watches.*

BACH (*with an edge to his voice*)....Remarkable.

I see it is entirely within your control.

FREDERICK *runs a hand caressingly across it.*

FREDERICK. I am completely infatuated by it. So much so, I have fifteen of them.

He shoots a look at CARL.

Why have one, when you can have twenty?

Beat. He turns to BACH.

One could say, it is ideally designed for your music, Herr Bach.

That the fortepiano needed to be invented to play Bach.

Beat.

BACH (*coldly*). Why?

FREDERICK (*smoothly*). To reveal the beautiful lines of your work, of course. Without volume control, on the harpsichord for instance, your music can sound like... a tangle. Confusion. Some parts *need* to be made subservient, some more dominant. Don't you think?

Silence. BACH's *face is expressionless.*

Try it.

Go on.

Unwillingly, BACH *sits down, plays a few phrases. Stops.*

FREDERICK.... What do you think?

BACH (*flatly*). The treble is frail and the keyboard action gouty, in my opinion.

Beat.

FREDERICK. I would like you to play all of them, before the night is out. All fifteen, if that would not exhaust you too much.

I would like to hear a great virtuoso play.

CARL, *eyeing* BACH *uneasily, interjects –*

CARL. My father is not well.

FREDERICK (*blithely*). A great virtuoso who will not be around for much longer, then.

– All the luckier for us, that you are here tonight.

Beat.

Please, sit, if you are tired after your long journey.

BACH. No need.

Now FREDERICK *addresses him intimately.*

FREDERICK. Tell me, Herr Bach. How would you define 'fugue'?

BACH *looks at him suspiciously.*

BACH.... Your Majesty needs no lessons from me.

FREDERICK. I see.

But I've heard you like argument. Arguments. In print, in person.

I must say, I rather like unison. People agreeing with me.

Your son is certainly a faithful disciple of yours in many ways. Do you think *he* believes in counterpoint?

BACH (*dismissively*). Of course Carl believes in counterpoint. I taught him.

FREDERICK *looks at* CARL *with relish.*

FREDERICK. *Do* you?

Beat.

CARL *says nothing. The mechanical cockerel suddenly crows, twice, a musical chiming.* BACH *stares at* CARL, *who won't meet his eye.*

But it's late. And we haven't even heard you play yet. Not really.

I would like to set you a little challenge.

He rests his hand on the pianoforte.

Before I do, let me ask you.

Herr Bach, do you believe everything can be made the subject of counterpoint?

BACH.…I do.

FREDERICK. Really?

BACH. Yes. Everything.

Just as everyone can be the subject of love.

FREDERICK *raises his eyebrows.*

FREDERICK. Ah. I'm not sure *that* is true!

We are not all lovable.

Some of us are not capable of being loved.

Wouldn't you say, Carl?

Beat. He goes to sit at the pianoforte.

Let me play you a subject for counterpoint, Herr Bach.

Twenty-one notes.

FREDERICK *plays, slowly, twenty-one notes.*

Then, there is silence. Slowly, BACH *begins to clap.*

BACH. Bravo.

This is…

Anti-contrapuntal brilliance.

Built to be as resistant to counterpoint as it is possible to be.

Descending in semitones, chromatic, it is so complex, so slippery it's obscene. Devilish.

Turning, he looks sharply at CARL.

Who composed it?

FREDERICK *(airily).* I haven't the *faintest* idea.

Beat.

I'd like you to execute it in a three-part fugue, please.

BACH *(drily).* Execute, you say?

FREDERICK. Yes. Now.

There is a slight intake of breath around the court.

Three voices.

Slowly, BACH *begins to play – the beginning of the Musical Offering. As the voices enter –*

BACH....Second voice...

He plays.

...Third voice...

FREDERICK *lets him play, until it is obvious* BACH *is able to meet the challenge.*

Then he interrupts.

FREDERICK. Oh, very nice. The old style we all so admire. Passing the melody from left hand to right like a skipping rope.

Yes yes yes. Stop.

BACH *stops playing.*

Now, for six voices, please.

BACH. Six.

FREDERICK. Yes. Six.

Silence.

BACH *stares at the keyboard.*

BACH. I can't.

FREDERICK. You can't?

Pause.

BACH....Not every subject is suitable for counterpoint.

FREDERICK (*triumphantly*). Are you saying that not all of us are suitable for love, Old Bach?

BACH....Perhaps.

FREDERICK. A defeat, then.

Beat.

BACH. You have no power over me unless it had been given you from above.

FREDERICK (*interested*). Of course...

You believe in God, in the soul.

Beat.

My view of life is that it is chaotic, accidental, and absolutely without meaning, a twisted clockwork in which we are all inanimate cogs. I go round like the wheel of a watermill simply because I am dragged that way. Men are stags, breeding to fill a field.

And yet you are right. I cannot wean myself of the idea that I have a soul.

Beat. He yawns.

I'm going to bed now.

Just before he exits:

Oh. I was sorry to hear about the death of your son Gottfried. I gather he turned up in Jena. Where he had enrolled, for some reason, to read law. Found dead of a hot fever.

My sincere condolences.

BACH *looks at him, stricken.*

CARL's *young son stares at* BACH, *fascinated.*

Music – Mass in B Minor, Kyrie Eleison.

Scene Five

BACH *sits in a chair. His eyes are bandaged.* ANNA *busies herself about the room. There is a long silence while* ANNA *quietly folds linen.*

BACH. What can I hear?

ANNA stops moving about, listens.

ANNA. I don't know.

BACH. ...It sounds like... breathing.

ANNA listens.

ANNA. Oh... Katharina... she's sleeping in the chair at the bottom of the stairs.

BACH. Ah.

ANNA. Goodness. She's two flights down.

Beat.

Your ears are incredible.

ANNA starts to move around again.

Are you working? While you sit there?

BACH. Yes. In my head.

She tenderly strokes the top of his head.

ANNA. I wish I could hear it.

BACH. You will.

Beat.

All these sounds. I want it all. Pennies down a well, water trickling, footsteps, and shapes, ribbons in and out of a corset...

ANNA. My darling.

There is faint singing from off.

There they go. The Sunday Cantata.

They listen.

What do you think?

BACH. I think... I fucking hate monks. They can't sing.

Beat. The singing stops. Birdsong.

Blackbird's been going crazy all morning.

ANNA. Nesting.

BACH. I had a canary once. Poor thing, it was blinded. To make it sing better.

Beat.

What I don't understand is why my right arm won't work.

Beat. He cranes his head towards her.

Anna.

She turns to him.

Why can't I like any of my sons' music?

ANNA....You are a person who can't lie.

BACH. That's not really an answer.

She strokes him, tenderly.

ANNA. My darling...

I fell in love with your energy, your restlessness, your bad temper.

She thinks.

(*To herself.*) I was the younger woman. Now I'm older than she was.

BACH....But why can't I give comfort? I can do it in my music.

Why can't I do it for them?

ANNA. Shhh.

Pause.

BACH. The candle is a stub.

ANNA. What?

BACH. The candle is a stub.

Pause. ANNA *now sees from the workings of his face that* BACH *is struggling with tears.*

ANNA. Bastian, what's wrong?

BACH. I've been blind. All along.

All I have now is doubt.

That I did the right thing.

I favoured him. And it ruined him.

What's the use of hearing everything?

He weeps.

Scene Six

ANNA *and* KATHARINA *stand with* CARL. CARL *is in travelling clothes.*

KATHARINA. Thank God you're here. Willy's determined to leave. Try and persuade him to stay.

CARL. How is Dad? Is he conscious still?

KATHARINA. In and out. Out, at the moment. He's not eating any more. But I got him to take some water, earlier.

ANNA. He suddenly decided to revise some music... he was dictating to Wilhelm, then to me. Then he seemed to fall asleep. Then Wilhelm said he was going to leave and that we couldn't stop him.

CARL. What piece?

ANNA. The Great Mass. He can't see anything any more.

CARL. Why?

ANNA. He had an operation. His eyesight was failing. Two months ago. It left him completely blind.

KATHARINA. That's not true. Ten days ago, he saw again. In the afternoon. First he saw the shape of the window. Then he saw the whole room. That's when he started work on the Mass.

ANNA. Katharina, it lasted for seconds. (*To* CARL.) He's blind. That doctor was a complete charlatan. He even insisted on operating twice to get double the fee. It was the second go that finished poor Bastian off. He has had seizure after seizure.

CARL. My God.

WILHELM *comes in. He stares at* CARL.

WILHELM. What are *you* doing here?

CARL. They told me he was dying.

WILHELM. ...How are you not ashamed?

ANNA. Wilhelm.

WILHELM. I heard. They told me. They're already advertising his job, the ungrateful cunts, and you auditioned for it. That's why you're here. In Leipzig. He isn't even dead yet!

CARL. No. I didn't.

WILHELM. You're revolting.

CARL. I can't talk to you sensibly if you're drunk.

WILHELM. I'm not drunk. Fucking... *lawyer*. Note-taker, penny-pincher, *thief*. You write religious music and you don't believe in God. You steal his music – I've heard it – you think we don't notice?

CARL. He gave us his music. At least I don't steal his money.

WILHELM. I don't steal his money. He gave me some. Once, a long time ago.

CARL. Yes. Then you started selling his music, instead. You lost his scores. You lost his St Matthew Passion –

WILHELM. You crucified him at court.

Pause.

Why the fuck are you here?

CARL. Because he's dying and I want to see him.

Beat.

WILHELM. Do what you want. I'm going.

ANNA. Willy.

CARL. Don't, Willy. He will want you there. If he's dying.

WILHELM. You've no right to tell me to stay when you fucked
off long ago.

CARL. Willy. Please.

Beat.

You need to stay. For his sake. He will want you.

You're the one he loves the most.

His favourite.

Pause. WILHELM *breaks down.*

WILHELM. I can't. I'm not strong enough. My whole life I've
been in the full glare of his love.

CARL *tries to hug him.* WILHELM *resists, then lets him.*

CARL. I heard they were trying to fill his job. I went to them. I
begged them to give it to you, or to me. It doesn't matter
who does it. The important thing is that it is passed on.
Family. It's what he would want.

WILHELM *angrily brushes away his tears.*

WILHELM. Poor Dad. Life is so unfair.

KATHARINA. No, Willy. He never wanted all that other stuff.

CARL (*to* WILHELM). You're looking at it the wrong way.
Everything contains its opposite. He wrote you the
Variations. The parts look separate on the page but it's an
illusion – your hands are all over each other, like crabs. Dad

was pious, and a shagger. He was stingy, and generous. I'm arrogant, and ashamed. Life is chaotic. But we make order out of it. Not God. We do. By behaving well. Even if that means a lie.

Stay.

WILHELM *cries*.

WILHELM. I can't. It's too painful.

CARL *takes hold of him, gently*.

CARL. It's okay. It's okay.

KATHARINA. God forgives.

Pause. WILHELM *detaches himself. Slowly, he walks out and leaves*.

ANNA. Go in to him, Carl.

Beat. CARL *leaves, and walks in the other direction, towards* BACH, *into the darkness of his bedroom. The others recede and disappear, leaving only* CARL *and* BACH, *now visible in his bed, on stage. Lit by one candle. Much weaker now. He no longer wears a bandage on his eyes but they are closed.*

CARL....Dad?

BACH....Who's there?

CARL. It's me. Carl.

Pause. Then BACH *slowly sings the opening notes of the Musical Offering*.

BACH. I sent it to him. His fugue in six voices. I did it. I just needed time.

I incorporated that damn imperial theme twelve times in a seventeen-minute piece. Back to front, upside down, inside out. And I dedicated it to him in German. So there.

CARL. I'm sorry, Father.

He starts to cry. Swallows his tears. Pause.

When I was little, I woke up with a nightmare. The room was dark and I told you, 'Daddy, my eyes aren't working.' You lit me a candle.

It was always you who came to me. Not Mummy, because she was with the baby.

It was you. Because you were always awake. Working.

Beat.

The craving for form in this chaos. I understand you now.

Pause.

BACH. You can help me. On the harpsichord there.

CARL *walks over, picks up a piece of sheet music.*

'Wenn wir in höchsten Nöten sein.'

CARL. 'When we are in the greatest distress.'

BACH. Willy was helping me. We were setting it to a different text.

A variation in counterpoint.

CARL. Let me find a quill.

He hunts about the room. Finds one. Sits near BACH.

I'm ready, Dad.

Pause.

BACH. Where's Willy?

CARL *starts to cry, silently again. Again, he swallows his tears.*

CARL. Wait a minute, Dad. I'll just go and get him.

He walks a few steps away, to the edge of the room. He comes back.

Dad? I'm here.

BACH *reaches out his hand. He touches CARL's face. Pause.*

BACH. I see.

Thank you, my son.

Pause.

There is a shape to all these things. Dissonance has to be resolved into harmony.

CARL *starts to cry again, silently.*

Don't cry, little one.

The love of your parents is like the music of the spheres. You can't hear it because it has always been there. From the moment of your birth.

He kisses CARL*'s hand.*

...I want to fix it.

We have time, Carl.

It will work for a different text. Vor deinen Thron.

CARL *readies his pen.* BACH *breathes in, and out again, with some difficulty.*

It's a prayer. The tempo should be the same as the heart. The struggle of the soul to leave the body.

Each bar a breath, a deep breath, in and out.

He breathes in, and out again.

It should be simple. Very simple.

Slowly, we hear the music: Vor deinen Thron – Gardiner choral arrangement.

CARL *starts to notate.*

Fade to black.

The End.

www.nickhernbooks.co.uk

 facebook.com/nickhernbooks

twitter.com/nickhernbooks